Moonology™

Diary 2025

Yasmin Boland

HAY HOUSE

HAY HOUSE

Carlsbad, California • New York City
London • Sydney • New Delhi

This diary belongs to

Published in the United Kingdom by:
Hay House UK Ltd, The Sixth Floor, Watson House,
54 Baker Street, London W1U 7BU
Tel: +44 (0)20 3927 7290; www.hayhouse.co.uk

Published in the United States of America by:
Hay House LLC, PO Box 5100, Carlsbad, CA 92018-5100
Tel: (1) 760 431 7695 or (800) 654 5126; www.hayhouse.com

Published in Australia by:
Hay House Australia Publishing Pty Ltd, 18/36 Ralph St, Alexandria NSW 2015
Tel: (61) 2 9669 4299; www.hayhouse.com.au

Published in India by:
Hay House Publishers India, Muskaan Complex, Plot No.3, B-2,
Vasant Kunj, New Delhi 110 070
Tel: (91) 11 4176 1620; www.hayhouse.co.in

A catalogue record for this book is available from the British Library.

ISBN: 978-1-78817-660-6

Interior images: vi: 123RF; all other images Creative Market and Shutterstock

This product uses responsibly sourced papers and/or recycled materials.
For more information, see www.hayhouse.co.uk

Printed and bound in Italy by Elcograf

FSC www.fsc.org MIX Paper from responsible sources FSC® C115118

Contents

Welcome to 2025!

This year, we're heading into uncharted waters. There are massive energy shifts coming our way, some of which haven't been seen for literally hundreds of years. So it's a year to throw away the past and whatever didn't work out for you, and see where you are now. Remember, it's in the present that you'll create your future – and this diary aims to help you do exactly that. Not to overstate it, but this diary contains the keys to the Universe!

Before we get into the detail of the energies of the year ahead and how to use them to shape your life, please let me remind you of *how* you can create your life. I say 'remind you' because, even if this is your first time reading a Moonology™ diary, on some level, you know that you're creating your life with your thoughts and emotions. This diary is designed to give you a guide to the energies coming at you, so to speak, to help you navigate and stay centered so you can make the most of the energetic portals opening up.

In a nutshell, this is what we do in Moonology™:

- Make wishes at New Moon
- Go for it in the waxing cycle (from New to Full Moon)

- Surrender it all to the Divine/release/forgive at Full Moon
- Let it all go in the waning cycle (from Full back to New Moon)

So you're aware, this process is based on the one month of the lunar cycle (the word 'month' actually shares roots with the word 'Moon' as well as the old-world word 'Moonth'). The Moon moves through the 12 zodiac signs (or Star signs) during each lunar cycle/month, and we get one New Moon and one Full Moon every month. Occasionally there are three New or Full Moons in a single month; the third Moon is known as a Blue Moon.

Moonology™ isn't something I invented (though I did coin and trademark the word!). Rather, it's a set of teachings drawn from many magical women and enlightened men who over the years have contributed to our understanding of how to work with the Moon and how the Moon works. Take a dash of the Burning Times, when women were burned at the stake for sharing this knowledge, add a flourish of magic from the women who still send out their spells at New Moon, call in some angels and Goddesses and a willingness to do what it takes to change your life, sprinkle in an understanding of the law of attraction, and you're on your way to what I've come to call Moon Manifesting (sometimes jokingly referred to as 'Moonifesting') to help you consciously create the life of your dreams.

What's Happening This Year and How Does It Help Me?

This year we have a total of 24 New and Full Moons – 12 of each. The year kicks off with the Full Moon in Cancer on January 13 and ends with the New Moon in Sagittarius on December 20.

So, to recap, that's:

- 12 chances to make your wishes and set your intentions
- 12 chances to make peace with what is, and release
- 12 chances to redirect yourself if you feel you've gone off course
- 12 chances to think about what really matters to you
- 12 chances to rewrite your life story

And a lot more!

But here's the thing: There's a lot of work to be done if you want to create your own reality. There are going to be times when it's harder than usual to do your Moonology™ work. There will be times when you're going through a difficult patch in your life and it's going to be challenging to maintain your faith that you're actually able to create, plan, and predict your life. Sometimes you're just going to be too busy. But if you want to change your life, you have to change life itself, so keep showing up.

In other words, don't just buy this diary, read this introduction, and then leave it on your pile of unread books and wonder why the magic isn't happening in your life. I've been working with the Moon for more than 20 years now and I've worked really hard to craft the information that I give you, hopefully paring it back as much as I possibly can so that you can do the bare minimum and still get amazing results.

Obviously, if you want to be a really good Moon student, you can take what I'm offering you here in this diary and run with it far and wide.

But first things first. Here's how to use this diary:

- **Every month** – check out the monthly overview (see *January on pages 26–27*) so you can get an idea of the upcoming energies in the weeks ahead.
- **Every New Moon** – use the space provided to write down your New Moon wishes and intentions (see *page 31 for an example*). Note that these pages ask you for action steps that you can take, so make sure you write them down and then do them!
- **Every Full Moon** – hop back in and make sure you answer the Full Moon questions (see *example on page 39*) about whatever you're releasing into the ethers.
- **Every week** – check the This Week page to see whether there is a New or Full Moon. If it's a Quarter Moon, be sure to take a moment to do a gratitude practice (more about that soon).
- **Every day** – you can use the small space provided for each day for appointments or to make a daily note of what you're grateful for, what you're feeling, your oracle or tarot card of the day, and so on.

By committing to working with the Moon through the year, you'll soon begin to understand why I believe that this diary contains the keys to the Universe!

Understanding the Lunar Cycle

Here's a quick guide to the nine main Moon phases – though you really only need to think about the New and Full Moons, with a dash of Quarter and Dark Moons thrown in. However, it's good to understand them all in the context of the whole monthly lunar cycle.

The New Moon: It's time to get clear and set some serious intentions. No vague wishes. Set clear goals and make proper commitments to yourself. Write them down!

The Waxing Crescent Moon: Put the pedal to the metal and take action on those intentions. This is the time to go full speed ahead and set things in motion.

The First Quarter Moon: Challenges can arise, but see them as an opportunity to recommit to your dreams. Face them head-on. Remind yourself how determined you are.

The Gibbous Moon: This phase is packed with expectations. *Don't* hold your breath!

The Full Moon: Emotional fireworks are possible at this time! What's been unclear is illuminated, including if your dreams are starting to manifest. Keep your eyes wide open. Surrender. Forgive. Release.

The Disseminating Moon: Take a breath and process everything you've been through.

The Last Quarter Moon: Let go of what didn't work out. This phase is all about shedding the excess baggage and freeing yourself from anything that's holding you back.

The Balsamic Moon: Get ready for some healing and soothing energy. Use this time to find peace within yourself and make peace with life itself.

The Dark Moon: This is a time for what's called 'kenosis' – a sacred and spiritual emptying-out. Let the past crumble away, allowing space for the New Moon phase with a clean and rejuvenated spirit.

The Moon cycles through these nine phases each month. She moves into a new astrological sign every two-and-a-bit days (this really is about as accurate as we can get!), and these sign changes are denoted on the daily diary pages. When you see two astrology symbols, the Moon has transitioned from the first sign to the second during that day. These are the 12 Star signs and their symbols:

Sign	Glyph	Sign	Glyph
Aries	♈	Libra	♎
Taurus	♉	Scorpio	♏
Gemini	♊	Sagittarius	♐
Cancer	♋	Capricorn	♑
Leo	♌	Aquarius	♒
Virgo	♍	Pisces	♓

On the 'This Week' page for each New and Full Moon, you'll find the degree at which that lunation occurs. To understand degrees, think of the zodiac as a 360-degree circle divided into 12 segments or signs. Each sign is made up of 30 degrees (expressed as 0–29 degrees). Each degree is further divided into 60 minutes, which are expressed from 0–59. So, for instance, the notation 09°Capricorn20′ means that the lunation occurs at nine degrees and 20 minutes in Capricorn. Once you start to know your horoscope chart and understand astrology, this becomes really interesting information, not least because it tells you whether or how a lunation is triggering one of your planets or points. If you don't understand this yet, please don't worry. (But if you do and you want to learn more about astrology, you can read my book *Astrology Made Easy*.)

The Importance of Gratitude

One thing we're ramping up in this year's diary is asking you to do a gratitude practice twice a month, at the First and Last Quarter Moons. If you do this, your life will almost certainly start to improve.

You can either simply fill out the page we have twice a month asking you to reflect on what you're grateful for, or you can take it to the next level and have a little gratitude session once every two weeks with family or friends (who will hopefully also have the diary!), be it online or in person. The idea is for everyone to talk about at least one thing they're grateful for. (I always love doing this on a Friday night once the week is done and dusted, when we can all be grateful and then have some drinks and nibbles!)

In other words, you don't have to be serious or studious about it. Have as much fun or as much sacred solitude as you want!

Beyond this, gratitude is going to be a major theme for this diary and this year. I'm going to help you to understand how your life will improve when you take a moment every couple of weeks, every week, or even every day to think about what you're grateful for and make a note of it or hold it in your mind.

Working with the Houses

In astrology and Moonology™, everyone has a horoscope chart. This is a 360-degree snapshot of the heavens at the time you were born, in the place you were born. This chart is divided into 12 sections, or Houses, with each one ruling a different part of your life. Here's a quick summary:

- **The 1st House:** your appearance and image; self-identity; how you come across to others
- **The 2nd House:** cash, property, and possessions; values, including how you value yourself
- **The 3rd House:** communications, siblings, neighbors, and quick trips; early education
- **The 4th House:** home, family, and all things domestic; where you belong; your past

- **The 5th House:** romance, creativity, and kids (your own or someone else's); pursuit of pleasure, love affairs
- **The 6th House:** daily routines, including those at work; your health; duty
- **The 7th House:** your lovers, spouse, ex, and open enemies; any partner, including business partners; cooperation and competition
- **The 8th House:** joint finances, credit cards, debts; sex and anything you consider taboo; inheritance, transformation
- **The 9th House:** study; travel; the Great Cosmic Quest; the Internet; higher learning; religion; spirituality; dreams
- **The 10th House:** your career and ambitions; how you make your mark on the world; what you're known for; reputation
- **The 11th House:** friends, networks, social circles, and what you're wishing for
- **The 12th House:** the deepest, darkest, most sensitive part of your chart; fears; spirituality; self-undoing; withdrawal

As the New and Full Moons move through the signs during the course of a year, they each trigger one House after another. To find out which part of your life is being triggered:

1. Turn to the page of the New or Full Moon in question, and read the section called How to Work with This Moon (see *page 30 for an example*).

2. Check out which House is being triggered depending on your Star sign or Rising sign (see *below*).
3. Find the interpretation for that House on the following pages.
4. Make plans based on what you read.

What's My Rising Sign?

Your Rising sign, also known as your Ascendant, is the zodiac sign that was coming up over the eastern horizon at the moment of your birth. It represents the way you come across in the world. It's not the real you (that's your Star sign, or zodiac sign), but rather the social mask you wear. You'll get far more accurate predictions and readings by working with your Rising sign.

If you don't yet know your Rising sign, your can cast your chart for free at my site (see *page 22*). Once you know your Rising sign, refer to the following pages to find out how each New and Full Moon will affect you in the year ahead.

What If I Don't Know My Time of Birth?

You need to know your specific location and time of your birth to determine your Rising sign. If you don't have that information, you can work with your Star sign (aka your zodiac sign). It might not be as accurate as your Rising sign, but if you work with all the 24 New and Full Moons of 2025, you'll have worked on every House in your chart and therefore on almost every part of your life.

The New Moon through the Houses

1st House

The New Moon is taking place in your sign this month, which is big news. It essentially offers you the chance to start again in any part of your life where you know it's needed. If you're really happy with the way things are going, it can just be an energy recharge. If you want to change the way others see you, the coming four weeks are the time to work on that. Ditto if you want to do something to change your basic appearance.

2nd House

This month, the New Moon is taking place in the part of your chart that's all about cash, property, and possessions, so it's the ideal time to start to make changes in those areas. Remember that money is energy, and it responds quite quickly to our thoughts of abundance or lack thereof. If you know you've been thinking negatively about cash, use this New Moon as a marker and decide that henceforth you'll turn your thoughts and expectations about cash around.

3rd House

When it comes to getting what we want, one of the other most important things we can do is very old-fashioned: communicate! Be it at work or in our personal life, it's so important to let others know what we want. The act of saying what we want invokes the law of attraction because speaking our desires means we need to have some conviction that we can get what we want. The New Moon this month in your Communication Zone brings energy galore to spend on communicating. What do you want? Who can help you? Just ask.

4th House

Your home life, your personal life, your domestic life, your past, your family, the people who feel like family, and your actual home – all these parts of your life are up for renewal now at this New Moon. If you haven't been getting on well at home or with your family, this is the ideal time to sort things out. At home, if you want to move, sell, or buy, or just change housemates, it's all extra possible. For some, there's a revelation connected to your past.

5th House

Welcome to the House of Fun! Have you been having a bit of that lately? If not, then the skies are strongly suggesting that it's time to get out and do a little bit of what you fancy! This New Moon offers a new start for you now regarding romance, creativity, and/or kids. Could you use a restart in these areas? Identify which one(s) you want to work on and draw up an action plan. Remember, the law of attraction means we can't get what we want until we know what we want.

6th House

Oh, you lucky, lucky thing! The New Moon is in your 6th House, the part of your chart that's all about your daily routines. That might not sound exactly riveting, but this is the part of your chart where you get a chance to tweak your routines so that your daily life runs in a more pleasing way, and eventually makes your life more functional and enjoyable. So, if there are minor changes you need to make to your routines and schedules, then this is a great month to put those changes in place.

7th House

How's your love life? This New Moon is happening in your Love Zone, which means you're getting the chance to reinvigorate your love life. If you're single, this is the perfect time to draw a line under the past and to move on from your old loves, your old dreams, and any old heartaches. If you're attached, you probably already know about the importance of keeping your relationship fresh – and this New Moon brings in the energy for that.

8th House

This New Moon is firing up the part of your chart that deals with sex and finances – sometimes separately and sometimes at the same time. When it comes to sex, if your love life is full, do whatever it takes to rev things up. If you've been inhibited, try something new. Go as far as you feel comfortable! Money-wise, it's all about where your money is involved with someone else, so you have a chance for a restart regarding your pay or salary. *Plus*, it's a very good time to set up a debt-repayment plan.

9th House

The New Moon this month will be in the part of your chart related to study, travel, adventure, and the Great Cosmic Quest. Just remember that you have a rush of new energy in all these parts of your life, so if you have plans in those areas, then you have the sky's support. This part of your chart is about seeing the big picture of your life and putting things in perspective. It's about higher learning and self-improvement. This is the month to open your eyes to the big, wide world rather than fretting about all the little details on the home front.

10th House

Let's hope you're feeling revved up about your career or studies because this month's New Moon is flooding your professional or student life with potential and ambition. If you're already on the right path, this lunation here can really amp things up. However, if you're struggling professionally and not quite sure where to turn, use this New Moon as a marker. Over the coming four weeks, thoroughly research your job market and put yourself out there by talking to experts who can help you get where you want to be career-wise.

11th House

The New Moon is taking place this month in your 11th House, which is the part of your chart that relates to your friends and the things you're wishing for. In a nutshell, having the New Moon here's very auspicious for two reasons. For one, it means you're in a cycle over the coming four weeks when you can meet new people, and sometimes that's the exact tonic we need. Be open to having new friends in your life. For another, though, it's a hugely important time for manifesting.

12th House

You're in a slightly strange cycle – can you feel it? This month, the New Moon is taking place in the part of your chart where you keep All Matters Hidden and Spiritual. This can be a time when you just want to withdraw from the world, but if you're into growing and evolving as your walk the spiritual path, this can be a time when you step away from the madness to meditate and contemplate, knowing that the Universe will deliver the messages you need to hear.

The Full Moon through the Houses

1st House

It's all very well and lovely to be focused on someone else, but once a year the Full Moon lights up your chart to remind you that you also need to focus on yourself – and that time is now. If you're a giver rather than a taker, this is your month to remember how to say yes when people offer to help you and to ask for help if you need it and you're not getting it. If you feel extra emotional during this cycle, try to deal with what comes up rather than running away from it.

2nd House

A balance is required between what you do for yourself financially and what you do for others. There's your income to be considered and your debts. There's your self-worth and what you think you're worth, and there's what others are going to pay you. If you're about to make a major purchase, then you're doing it at the right time. If you've been letting someone control you because they have financial power over you, then this is your chance to break free. This Full Moon is also reminding you that you need to take care of your intimate life.

3rd House

This Full Moon is reminding you that there's a lot of work to be done close to home, things need to be taken care of, and there are items on your to-do list to be ticked. It's also a celestial reminder that you seriously need to express yourself – if you haven't been honest about how you feel, now is the time to start to say your piece, whether you're talking, Facebooking, emailing, tweeting, or whatever. Drama with siblings is highlighted and can be sorted now too.

4th House

When the Full Moon is in your 4th House, you're entering a four-week cycle when the Sun and the Moon are suggesting that you need to find a balance between your outer goals and your inner needs. Perhaps your family needs you to spend more time with them. Or perhaps you just need some time with nothing on your mind. Take a look at whether everything is running as smoothly as you'd like within your family relationships. If not, this is the time to pour some energy into that part of your life.

5th House

This Full Moon is taking place in the part of your chart related to self-expression. There's probably a whole lot of emotion going on in your life right now. This might be about pouring your heart out – because you're sad, or you have a lot of emotions to download. For others, it's about the joy that a child brings you; or it could be about pouring emotion into a creative project. Between all this, you need to find a balance between your Self and your friends. Don't neglect them totally. This is your challenge for the coming month.

6th House

If you're one of the lucky ones, this is the Full Moon when you see yourself for who you *really* are and therefore see your good points as well as your flaws – and you decide to do something about your flaws. This is all about the daily life you lead. Are you living in a healthy fashion? If not, then this Full Moon is your annual chance to start again when it comes to taking care of yourself, body, mind, and spirit. Routines are your friend now. At work, go slow and steady.

7th House

When the Full Moon is in your 7th House, it might be time for you to step aside and invest some emotional energy into either your other half or other people in general. 'Me, me, me' is fine at the right time, but right now it should be all about someone else. At the very least, there needs to be a balance. The Full Moon can also bring closures, so if you're in a friendship or relationship that's ending now, you can proceed knowing that you're finishing things up at the exact right time, celestially speaking.

8th House

This Full Moon is all about finding a balance between give and take. If you know you've been doing too much of either, it's time to redress the balance. The problem is that when we give too much but we don't know how to take, we mess with the natural laws that govern free flow. How can the Universe send you an abundant stream of good things if you're not receiving them without a fight? Now is a very good time to attend to practical financial matters.

9th House

Personal growth, religion, philosophy, publishing, the Internet, travel, and study – these are just some of the subjects looming large for you at this Full Moon. Be honest with yourself. Have you been fussing too much over the details of your latest problem or task? Sometimes that's just a delay tactic, and you need to take a step back and look at the big picture. Are your life and mind expanding or narrowing? If you've stopped being adventurous, then this is a great time to try something that's out of your usual realm of the everyday.

10th House

If you've been hiding yourself away and generally keeping a low profile, watch out! The skies are suggesting rather loudly that it's time for you to step out of the shadows and back into the limelight. As tempting as it might be to slouch around at home, this Full Moon is telling you to invest some energy into your professional life. For some, a work situation or project comes to an end now. Don't panic. Remember, the Universe abhors a vacuum, and something new will arrive in its place soon. How committed are you to your goals?

11th House

Of course, it's as tempting for you as it is for everyone else to focus on yourself and your own pleasures. Why shouldn't you express yourself? Of course you should! Life is for living and having fun. However, this month's Full Moon is reminding you that you need to find a balance between indulging yourself and remembering that the people in your life also need some attention – from you. Doing something for someone else will you get extra karmic Brownie points.

12th House

Life has probably felt very busy recently, and no one can blame you for wanting to take some time out. This Full Moon will allow you to do just that. If it comes at a time when you're feeling a little bit down in the dumps, the fact is, you're probably not down in the dumps per se; you're probably just exhausted after the efforts of keeping up with the demands of daily life. Take some time out. If you know how to meditate or do yoga, go for it. You need to strike a balance between working and resting.

The Moonology of 2025

Included in the 24 New and Full Moons of 2025 (and 25 Quarter Moons), are two Full Moon eclipses, which occur when the Earth, Moon and Sun are all in alignment and the Earth's shadow falls on the face of the Moon, and two New Moon eclipses, which occur when the Moon passes between the Sun and the Earth and obscures the face of the Sun.

Eclipses have been thin on the ground in the past few years. Every year we get a minimum of four eclipses and a maximum of seven; this year we have four. Eclipses are hot times; they're when the Universe changes gear. If they hit your chart strongly, they can affect you in a life-changing (and hopefully positively!) way.

Each New and Full Moon and eclipse has an overall flavor, which I'll go into in more detail in the sections devoted to them in their relevant month. You'll also find a list of key words and ideas for each lunation. These are the eclipses of 2025 (all times given are in UTC, or Universal Time Coordinated):

Lunar or solar eclipse?	Total or partial	Date	Sign	Time	Degrees
Lunar	Total	March 14	Virgo	06:54:36	23°Virgo56′
Solar	Partial	March 29	Aries	10:57:47	09°Aries00′
Lunar	Total	September 7	Pisces	18:08:50	15°Pisces22′
Solar	Partial	September 21	Virgo	19:54:04	29°Virgo05′

Major Planetary Moves

Although we focus on Moonology in this diary, it's also useful to know about the general astrological backdrop for the year – and this is another big one. We're sailing into uncharted waters, because *four* of the major planets are changing signs this year.

Here's a quick table of the changes happening. Note that the last three lines show Saturn, Neptune and Uranus retrograding into the signs they were in earlier in the year. You don't *need* to understand this, but I'll explain more as the year progresses.

Planetary move	Date	What this change brings
Neptune into Aries	March 30	Mystical experiences and confusion
Saturn into Aries	May 25	Lessons and stability
Jupiter into Cancer	June 9	Good luck, expansion, and arrogance
Uranus into Gemini	July 7	Both chaos and liberation
Saturn back into Pisces	September 1	More chances for spiritual lessons
Neptune back into Pisces	October 22	Spiritual reconnection
Uranus back into Taurus	November 8	Chaos in the money markets

Jupiter, Saturn, Uranus, and Neptune are four of the most impactful planets, so having them all changing signs this year means huge energy shifts. When these moves occur, make sure you:

1. Check out your birth chart to determine which House is ruled by which sign. If you haven't yet cast your chart, you can do it for free at my site (*see below*).

2. Work out what the sign of the planetary move governs for you. For example, when Neptune moves into Aries, look at the How to Work with This Moon section for the New Moon in Aries lunation (*see page 82*). Then find that House in The New Moon through the Houses section (*see pages 11–15*) to discover what it means for you. Neptune will be bringing you Neptunian, mystical experiences and/or confusion in the part of your life (House) mentioned. And Saturn will be bringing you lessons and stability. I have an explainer video about this on my site if you'd like to learn more about this (*see below*).

Resources

I've created lots of great resources to support you on your manifesting journey in the year ahead.

- To cast your chart for free, visit: www.moonmessages.com/freechart

- For the Diary Bonuses Area, explainer videos, meditations, and more, visit: www.moonmessages.com/diary

Have an amazing 2025 – we're off to the Moon!

Yasmin

Weekly Diary

JANUARY						
M	T	W	T	F	S	S
		1	2	3	4	5
6	7	8	9	10	11	12
13	14	15	16	17	18	19
20	21	22	23	24	25	26
27	28	29	30	31		

FEBRUARY						
M	T	W	T	F	S	S
					1	2
3	4	5	6	7	8	9
10	11	12	13	14	15	16
17	18	19	20	21	22	23
24	25	26	27	28		

MARCH						
M	T	W	T	F	S	S
					1	2
3	4	5	6	7	8	9
10	11	12	13	14	15	16
17	18	19	20	21	22	23
24	25	26	27	28	29	30
31						

APRIL						
M	T	W	T	F	S	S
	1	2	3	4	5	6
7	8	9	10	11	12	13
14	15	16	17	18	19	20
21	22	23	24	25	26	27
28	29	30				

MAY						
M	T	W	T	F	S	S
			1	2	3	4
5	6	7	8	9	10	11
12	13	14	15	16	17	18
19	20	21	22	23	24	25
26	27	28	29	30	31	

JUNE						
M	T	W	T	F	S	S
						1
2	3	4	5	6	7	8
9	10	11	12	13	14	15
16	17	18	19	20	21	22
23	24	25	26	27	28	29
30						

JULY						
M	T	W	T	F	S	S
	1	2	3	4	5	6
7	8	9	10	11	12	13
14	15	16	17	18	19	20
21	22	23	24	25	26	27
28	29	30	31			

AUGUST						
M	T	W	T	F	S	S
				1	2	3
4	5	6	7	8	9	10
11	12	13	14	15	16	17
18	19	20	21	22	23	24
25	26	27	28	29	30	31

SEPTEMBER						
M	T	W	T	F	S	S
1	2	3	4	5	6	7
8	9	10	11	12	13	14
15	16	17	18	19	20	21
22	23	24	25	26	27	28
29	30					

OCTOBER						
M	T	W	T	F	S	S
		1	2	3	4	5
6	7	8	9	10	11	12
13	14	15	16	17	18	19
20	21	22	23	24	25	26
27	28	29	30	31		

NOVEMBER						
M	T	W	T	F	S	S
					1	2
3	4	5	6	7	8	9
10	11	12	13	14	15	16
17	18	19	20	21	22	23
24	25	26	27	28	29	30

DECEMBER						
M	T	W	T	F	S	S
1	2	3	4	5	6	7
8	9	10	11	12	13	14
15	16	17	18	19	20	21
22	23	24	25	26	27	28
29	30	31				

January

December 30/31: Black New Moon in Capricorn

January 6/7: First Quarter Moon in Aries

January 13/14: Full Moon in Cancer

January 21/22: Last Quarter Moon in Scorpio

January 29: New Moon in Aquarius

Just when you thought you'd done all your letting go of the past and of 2024, along comes January 2025 with a challenge: Are you sure you're through all that s***? As the New Year dawns, I'd love to be able to tell you it's all roses, but the fact is we have one of the most challenging planetary alignments to deal with on January 3, as Mars (anger) clashes with Pluto (fury). And if you think that sounds like a recipe for a little bit of hotheadedness, you're right! So what to do?

For a start, just know that as we move into the new year, there could be some tensions. Forewarned is forearmed. What's the point of reading about the upcoming astrology if you don't use the information, right? So just be extra careful if, as 2025 begins, you find yourself feeling annoyed with someone. This too shall pass, and least said, soonest mended, as the sayings go.

Moreover, note that Mars is currently retrograde, which means a couple of things: 1) This is actually a replay of the alignment that took place in early November 2024, so unresolved issues that you're feeling angry about might come back up. Ideally, you worked out how to deal with these issues last year and this time around you can work through them more smoothly. 2) Note that power struggles can arise now, so act accordingly (ideally, dig as deep as you can and find a win:win solution any time issues come up). Later this month Mars' meeting with spiritual Neptune means that spiritual practices such as meditation and chanting can be helpful.

This month I will:

- ❑ **Meditate every day**
- ❑ **Work on my anger issues**
- ❑ **Release the past**

Black New Moon in Capricorn

KEY WORDS AND IDEAS FOR THIS LUNATION:

- Purification
- More lessons
- Setting intentions
- Feeling ambitious

DATE AND TIME OF THIS NEW MOON

LA: Dec 30, 14:26 | New York: Dec 30, 17:26 | London: Dec 30, 22:26 | Sydney: Dec 31, 09:26

After the difficult astrology of the last couple of weeks, this last New Moon of 2024 is positive overall. It's also what's known as a 'Black' New Moon, which just means it's a second New Moon in a calendar month. However, there's no real astrological significance other than getting twice the number of chances to make our New Moon wishes ahead of the new year.

This New Moon takes place in Capricorn, the sign ruled by Saturn. Saturn loves nothing more than to make a plan.

Under the Capricorn New Moon this week, set aside some time to make some New Moon/2025 intentions. Even if you're anti-New Year's resolutions, think of them as New Moon in Capricorn aims.

What do you want to achieve in the coming 12 months? The clearer you are about what you want to achieve, the more likely you are to achieve it.

The New Moon takes place just before Pluto connects with the lunar nodes, and is accompanied by a strong sense of purification. It's time to move on from the past. Burn it up in your mind. Forgive it. And then decide what you want to bring into your life to take the place of whatever you've cleared out.

This might sound like just a little exercise in a diary, but if you do it correctly, it can be life-changing. Getting clear on what you want is the first step to achieving it. Happily, this New Moon also has a constructive feeling to it, thanks to its harmonious alignment with Saturn, so healing is in the air.

'I AM' Exercise

Instead of writing down an endless list of all the things you want to achieve under this ambitious New Moon in Capricorn, try writing down statements beginning with the words 'I AM' as you talk about what you want to achieve. According to New Thought author Neville Goddard, doing this is one of the most powerful ways to get in touch with your inner divinity, which will help you manifest whatever you say you are. Not sure what to write? You could try: *I am happy, I am healthy, I am wealthy, and I am wise.* Say it and believe it!

How to Work with This Moon

To discover where the energy of this Black New Moon is for you, find your Star sign or Rising sign here, see which House is involved, and then read The New Moon through the Houses (see *pages 12–15*): Aries – 10th House; Taurus – 9th House; Gemini – 8th House; Cancer – 7th House; Leo – 6th House; Virgo – 5th House; Libra – 4th House; Scorpio – 3rd House; Sagittarius – 2nd House; Capricorn – 1st House; Aquarius – 12th House; Pisces – 11th House.

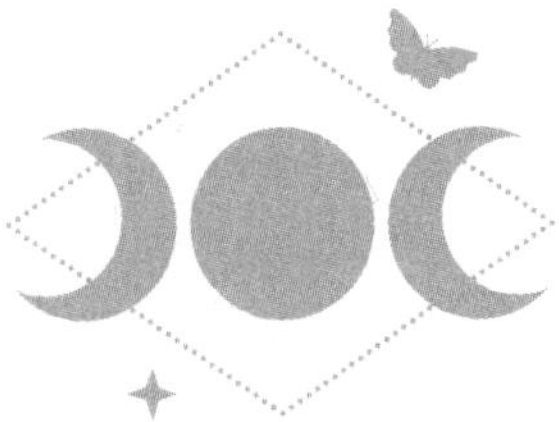

NEW MOON WISHES AND INTENTIONS

Thinking ahead to 2025, my current biggest, most audacious goal, wish, or intention is:

Now, turn it into an affirmation. Write it here as if it's already happened, and keep repeating it until the Full Moon.

Action steps I'm going to take toward this goal:

In the next 24 hours

In the coming week

In the month ahead

Tip: Write these actions as reminders on the diary pages.

I commit to this goal wholeheartedly!

Sign here:

This Week

The last New Moon of the year is happening. Use it to set some intentions for the year ahead, even if you 'don't believe' in resolutions! There's a huge power in doing this.

December 30/31: Black New Moon occurs at 09°Capricorn44'

January 3: Venus into Pisces; Mars clashes with Pluto

Quote of the Week

'Anger, if not restrained, is frequently more hurtful to us than the injury that provokes it.'

Seneca

December 2024–January 2025 – Week 1

30 Monday

New Moon: LA: 14:26 | New York: 17:26 | London: 22:26 ♐♑

31 Tuesday

New Moon: Sydney: 09:26 ♑

1 Wednesday

♑♒

2 Thursday

♒

3 Friday

♒♓

4 Saturday

♓

5 Sunday

♓♈

This Week

This could be a rather confusing week, but don't try too hard to make sense of things just yet. Clarity will come later. If you think someone is trying to trick you, be on your guard.

January 6: Mars into Cancer

January 6/7: First Quarter Moon occurs at 16°Aries56′

January 8: Mercury into Capricorn

What Are You Grateful For This Week?

January 2025 – Week 2

6 Monday

First Quarter Moon ♈ ◐

7 Tuesday

First Quarter Moon ♈ ♉ ◐

8 Wednesday

♉ ◐

9 Thursday

♉ ◐

10 Friday

♉ ♊ ◐

11 Saturday

♊ ◯

12 Sunday

♊ ♋ ◯

Full Moon in Cancer

KEY WORDS AND IDEAS FOR THIS LUNATION:

- Getting feisty
- Feeling emotional
- Anger rising
- Raging

DATE AND TIME OF THIS FULL MOON

LA: Jan 13, 14:26 | New York: Jan 13, 17:26 | London: Jan 13, 22:26 | Sydney: Jan 14, 09:26

Ooh, la la! The first Full Moon of the year is packing a punch! For one thing, it's taking place in the super-emotional sign of Cancer. Cancer is a Water sign, and Water is all about the emotions. Plus, the Moon is about emotions and feelings anyway. And if that weren't enough, this Full Moon is taking place near the planet of anger and ire, Mars, which, on top of everything else, is retrograde right now. Add all that up and it's fair to say that 2025 is starting with a bang! Is this a good thing? It can be.

If you're starting the year really wanting to move on from the past, this lunation will help. However, if you're trying to stay calm and keep life flowing smoothly, you'll have to try extra hard this month!

One of the good things about this Full Moon is that it's harmonizing with the planet of dreams and poetry, Neptune. So even if you're seeing red and feeling angrier than you'd like to, it's still possible to tune out of Mars' fire and ire and any old arguments that might resurface as a result. Instead, tune in to Neptunian calm using a spiritual practice such as meditation, yoga, chanting, breathwork, EFT (Emotional Freedom Technique), or whatever works for you.

We really do have to take responsibility for our emotions, even when we feel like the Universe is prodding and provoking us – and this is one of those times. By working with the Moon throughout the year ahead I hope you'll learn that there is rarely a good time to resist your feelings. Instead, process them as they arise to take better care of them!

Release Drama through Tapping

Have you heard of EFT (Emotional Freedom Technique), aka tapping? I'm a huge fan of it. It's a practice where you tap on certain points on the body to release drama from your energetic self. If you've never heard of it, visit my site (see *page 22*) for an explainer video. We have a few free resources there to help you get started.

Try saying something like this as you tap on the points: 'Even though 2025 is starting so intensely, and I'm feeling wound up about <insert whatever you're wound up about> and I need to breathe and it's hard, I truly and completely love and approve of myself.' Not feeling tense? Lucky you! Share this with someone you love who is.

How to Work with This Moon

To discover where the energy of this Full Moon is for you, find your Star sign or Rising sign here, see which House is involved, and then read The Full Moon through the Houses (see *pages 16–19*): Aries – 4th House; Taurus – 3rd House; Gemini – 2nd House; Cancer – 1st House; Leo – 12th House; Virgo – 11th House; Libra – 10th House; Scorpio – 9th House; Sagittarius – 8th House; Capricorn – 7th House; Aquarius – 6th House; Pisces – 5th House.

FULL MOON FORGIVENESS AND QUESTIONS TO ASK

It's very interesting that the year is beginning on such an intense note in terms of the Full Moon. Clearly, it means that humanity has a lot of anger to release at the moment! One of the best ways to get in touch with what you need to release is to answer these questions.

What upset(s) do I need to release from 2024?

What will happen if I stay angry or upset about this?

What would my life look like if I could release this?

This Week

The first Full Moon of the year looks like a hot one! In other words, don't be surprised if you find yourself feeling your feelings very intensely. That's okay! Just breathe.

January 13/14: Full Moon occurs at 24°Cancer00'

January 19: Sun into Aquarius

Quote of the Week

'I let go of all expectations. People, places, and things are free to be themselves, and I am free to be me.'

Louise Hay

January – Week 3

13 Monday

Full Moon: LA: 14:26 | New York: 17:26 | London: 22:26 ♋ ○

14 Tuesday

Full Moon: Sydney: 09:26 ♋ ♌ ○

15 Wednesday

♌ ○

16 Thursday

♌ ♍ ○

17 Friday

♍ ○

18 Saturday

♍ ◑

19 Sunday

♍ ♎ ◑

This Week

After a pretty intense start to the year, the energies calm down a little, which means we can as well! We're in the waning cycle now, so relax and breathe out.

January 21/22: Last Quarter Moon occurs at 02°Scorpio03'

What Are You Grateful For This Week?

January – Week 4

20 Monday

♎ ◑

21 Tuesday

Last Quarter Moon ♎ ♏ ◑

22 Wednesday

Last Quarter Moon ♏ ◑

23 Thursday

♏ ◑

24 Friday

♏ ♐ ◑

25 Saturday

♐ ◑

26 Sunday

♐ ♑ ●

New Moon in Aquarius

KEY WORDS AND IDEAS FOR THIS LUNATION:

- Powerful words
- Luck is in the air
- Second chances
- Inspiring love

DATE AND TIME OF THIS NEW MOON

LA: Jan 29, 04:35 | New York: Jan 29, 07:35 | London: Jan 29, 12:35 | Sydney: Jan 29, 23:35

It's the first New Moon of the year, so for our first-time diary users, let's take a moment to remind ourselves what the New Moon is all about and how to make the most of it.

This year is going to bring 12 New Moons. Each one of them is a chance to take a moment to get clear about what you actually want in your life. By doing that, you start to move into a space where not only do you know what you want, but you start to take the steps you need to in order to create it.

This is one of the things that the diary helps you with the most. Each month, you'll be asked what steps you need to take in the coming 24 hours, the next week, and the month ahead to achive your current biggest goal, wish, or intention. Taking action is crucial when you're manifesting.

Some people prefer to call this New Moon wishing or New Moon magic, and other people call it getting clear on your goals and taking action. Whatever you choose to call it is up to you. You just need to know that it's a core part of the magic of Moonology.

This New Moon has some very positive alignments. There could be lucky breaks thanks to a Jupiter alignment, and Venus/Neptune bring romance to the air for anyone who's making wishes to do with a relationship.

Do watch out, though, if you suspect your partner is up to no good. Neptune can be as deceptive as it is blissful.

Close Your Eyes and Make a Wish!

It's easy to live in a Moonology™ bubble and assume that everybody knows how to make New Moon wishes, but that's not the case. In fact, it seems as though the world is waking up. More and more people are starting to realize that we humans really do create our own reality. So the idea with the New Moon is to take a moment to get really clear on what you want. Sometimes it's not what you think. Once you know what you want, write it all down and visualize it, and turn it into an affirmation. How will you feel when your wish comes true? Feeling that feeling is the key to New Moon wishing success.

How to Work with This Moon

To discover where the energy of this New Moon is for you, find your Star sign or Rising sign here, see which House is involved, and then read The New Moon through the Houses (see *pages 12–15*): Aries – 11th House; Taurus – 10th House; Gemini – 9th House; Cancer – 8th House; Leo – 7th House; Virgo – 6th House; Libra – 5th House; Scorpio – 4th House; Sagittarius – 3rd House; Capricorn – 2nd House; Aquarius – 1st House; Pisces – 12th House.

NEW MOON WISHES AND INTENTIONS

My current biggest, most audacious goal, wish, or intention for 2025 is:

Now turn it into an affirmation. Write it here as if it's already happened, and keep repeating it until the Full Moon – and indeed all year until it manifests or you change your mind.

Action steps I'm going to take toward this goal:

In the next 24 hours

In the coming week

In the month ahead

Tip: Write these actions as reminders on the diary pages.

I commit to this goal wholeheartedly!

Sign here:

This Week

This is a week with a lot of potential for amazing chats where you can think with your head rather than lead with your heart, or just decide to put on some rose-tinted glasses!

January 28: Mercury enters Aquarius; Dark Moon

January 29: New Moon occurs at 09°Aquarius51′

January 30: Uranus retrograde ends

Quote of the Week

'Believe that life is worth living, and your belief will help create the fact.'

William James

January–February – Week 5

27 Monday

♑

28 Tuesday

♑ ♒

29 Wednesday

New Moon: LA: 04:35 | New York: 07:35 | London: 12:35 | Sydney: 23:35 ♒

30 Thursday

♒ ♓

31 Friday

♓

1 Saturday

♓

2 Sunday

♓ ♈

February

February 5: First Quarter Moon in Taurus

February 12/13: Full Moon in Leo

February 20/21: Last Quarter Moon in Sagittarius

February 27/28: New Moon in Pisces

The month starts off with a lovely romantic vibe as the planet of love, Venus, meets the planet of soulmates, Neptune. So, if you have your head in the clouds over someone, lucky you! However, do also be aware that this alignment can mean we all have our rose-tinted glasses on. In other words, you may not be able to see through the romantic fog – this applies especially if you're single and looking or attached but suspect your partner might not be all they seem. If you're with someone you adore and trust, dive into the romantic vibe. Also, on February 4, there's a Mars/Chiron clash – so if you've been trusting the wrong people (personally or professionally), that could be when the slap in the face with some painful reality comes.

Often a month will offer up a sort of 'overall narrative,' in that it's quite clear there's some kind of theme playing out, giving us lessons that we all need to learn. But this isn't really one of those months, apart from the fact that it does have romantic energy at the start, and of course mid-month brings Valentine's Day. Speaking of which, if you have a bumpy time in the lead-up to February 14, try not to panic. Make 'live and let live' your motto, and V-Day itself could be lovely, whether you spend it with your partner, someone who has potential, a bunch of friends or one friend, or alone. Do believe in love, but don't be too shortsighted!

February 24 brings the end of Mars retrograde, at which point life will start speeding up again.

This month I will:

- ☐ **Love love**
- ☐ **Believe in luck**
- ☐ **Get back on track**

This Week

Don't let someone's anger spoil your fun. Find the people who make you smile and hang out with them.

February 4: Venus into Aries; Jupiter goes direct

February 5: First Quarter Moon occurs at 16°Taurus46′

What Are You Grateful For This Week?

February – Week 6

3 Monday

4 Tuesday

5 Wednesday

First Quarter Moon

6 Thursday

7 Friday

8 Saturday

9 Sunday

Full Moon in Leo

KEY WORDS AND IDEAS FOR THIS LUNATION:

- Say what you mean
- Mean what you say
- Say goodbye if it's time
- Don't be too proud

DATE AND TIME OF THIS FULL MOON

LA: Feb 12, 05:53 | New York: Feb 12, 08:53 | London: Feb 12, 13:53 | Sydney: Feb 13, 00:53

This month's Full Moon is taking place in the sign of Leo. If you don't know anything about Leo, here's a crash course: it's the sign that rules the Sun; it thinks the Universe (or at least the solar system) revolves around it; and it's prideful, generous, magnanimous, and confident. In practice, this means:

If you've been too proud to let someone know how you feel or what you want, or if you've been too scared to try something because you fear looking silly if you fail, this Full Moon can be the perfect time to drop the pride and ego and go for it.

Additionally, because this Full Moon is triggering the communications planet Mercury, it's the perfect time to change everything with one conversation. Moreover, the Full Moon is making a harmonious alignment to lucky Jupiter, so the heavens are on your side whatever you decide to do now.

Just be careful you don't say too much because the next planetary alignment after the Full Moon is a clash between communications planet Mercury and the ebullient and sometimes-over-the-top planet Jupiter.

This lunation takes place just before Valentine's Day, which is a mixed blessing. Its high intensity means some lovers may feel a little over-wrought around the time of the Full Moon on 12 and 13 February. If you can get through these few days, the day and night of 14 February should flow!

Say What You Mean and Mean What You Say

In the spirit of the energy of this Full Moon, think about who you most need to have a conversation with. Perhaps it's someone you know really well, or someone you've just met. Maybe it's someone you work with or who lives down the road, etc. What do you need to say to them? If you can't summon the courage to speak up, grab your phone, hit the record button, and talk. Try to talk for at least 5 or 10 minutes. Just wax lyrical. See what comes to you. Speak with confidence, knowing that nobody ever has to hear the conversation apart from you. Then listen back. Make some notes. What have you realized about this situation as a result of this easy but meaningful exercise?

How to Work with This Moon

To discover where the energy of this Full Moon is for you, find your Star sign or Rising sign here, see which House is involved, and then read The Full Moon through the Houses (see *pages 16–19*): Aries – 5th House; Taurus – 4th House; Gemini – 3rd House; Cancer – 2nd House; Leo – 1st House; Virgo – 12th House; Libra – 11th House; Scorpio – 10th House; Sagittarius – 9th House; Capricorn – 8th House; Aquarius – 7th House; Pisces – 6th House.

FULL MOON FORGIVENESS AND QUESTIONS TO ASK

If you're new to working with Moonology™, then you might not know that every Full Moon we work on forgiveness. That's because at the time of the Full Moon our emotions rise, making it the best time to feel them, process them, and release them.

Have you been too proud to let someone know how you really feel? If so, what are you going to do about that?

Talking things through is highly recommended at the Full Moon. Who do you most need to have a conversation with to clear the air, and are you willing to make the first move?

Leo is packed with energy and confidence. How can you use that as you release anything that no longer serves you?

This Week

As if on cue, the planet of communications, Mercury, moves into the sign of soulmates, Pisces, on Valentine's Day – all the better to let that person know you've been admiring them!

February 12/13: Full Moon occurs at 24°Leo06′

February 14: Mercury moves into Pisces

Quote of the Week

'Love does not consist of gazing at each other, but in looking together in the same direction.'

ANTOINE DE SAINT-EXUPÉRY

February – Week 7

10 Monday

♋♌○

---

11 Tuesday

♌○

---

12 Wednesday

Full Moon: LA: 05:53 | New York: 08:53 | London: 13:53 ♌○

---

13 Thursday

Full Moon: Sydney: 00:53 ♌♍○

---

14 Friday

♍○

---

15 Saturday

♍♎○

---

16 Sunday

♎○

This Week

The Sun moves into Pisces this week, so life should start to feel a little less electric and a little more gentle. Speak kindly and don't say too much, and all should be well.

February 18: Sun into Pisces

February 20/21: Last Quarter Moon occurs at 02°Sagittarius20'

What Are You Grateful For This Week?

February – Week 8

17 Monday

♎

---

18 Tuesday

♎ ♏

---

19 Wednesday

♏

---

20 Thursday

Last Quarter Moon ♏ ♐

---

21 Friday

Last Quarter Moon ♐

---

22 Saturday

♐ ♑

---

23 Sunday

♑

New Moon in Pisces

KEY WORDS AND IDEAS FOR THIS LUNATION:

- Fantasy meets reality
- Dreams made real
- Second chances in love
- Meditate, meditate, meditate

DATE AND TIME OF THIS NEW MOON

LA: Feb 27, 16:44 | New York: Feb 27, 19:44 | London: Feb 28, 00:44 | Sydney: Feb 28, 11:44

This New Moon is taking place in the sign of dreams and soulmates, Pisces, and throwing out a challenge to us all to look on the bright side and to believe in our dreams. However, there's an undercurrent, too: we're being urged us to see what happens when we expect the best rather than the worst. Reason being, the New Moon is clashing with the planet of positivity, Jupiter, while also taking place quite near to the planet of pessimism, Saturn.

It's time to hope and believe your dreams can come true; just don't paper over any cracks. Ultimately, the energies are positive so do expect good things.

Jupiter is the planet of plenty, and even though this New Moon is clashing with Jupiter, as the world's leading astrologer, Robert Hand, once said to me: 'There's no such thing as a bad Jupiter transit.'

If you're finding one of your relationships – personal or professional – challenging, do what you can to make it better with an optimistic attitude, but also take reality into account. Be happy and optimistic, but know where to draw the line and don't accept the unacceptable.

Overall, this is very much a New Moon to ask yourself: *What really matters to me, and am I living my life in accordance with that?*

Also note that just after the New Moon, the planet of love and abundance, Venus, goes into one of her rare retrogrades. They happen about once every 18 months, and this one will last until mid-April. Between now and then, expect chances to make up with someone if you've fallen out but you still care.

What Really Matters?

This is one of my favorite exercises to do when Venus goes retrograde. Venus is all about what we really value. As such, when she starts to go retrograde, it's time to work out what really matters most to you. Once you're clear on that, start to live in a way that supports your priorities. Reevaluate everything, if need be. How? Simply grab a pen and paper, and off the top of your head write down the top-five most important things to you. Are you living your life in accordance with them?

How to Work with This Moon

To discover where the energy of this New Moon is for you, find your Star sign or Rising sign here, see which House is involved, and then read The New Moon through the Houses (see *pages 12–15*): Aries – 12th House; Taurus – 11th House; Gemini – 10th House; Cancer – 9th House; Leo – 8th House; Virgo – 7th House; Libra – 6th House; Scorpio – 5th House; Sagittarius – 4th House; Capricorn – 3rd House; Aquarius – 2nd House; Pisces – 1st House.

NEW MOON WISHES AND INTENTIONS

My current biggest, most audacious goal, wish, or intention is:

Now turn it into an affirmation. Write it here as if it's already happened, and keep repeating it until the Full Moon.

Action steps I'm going to take toward this goal:

In the next 24 hours

In the coming week

In the month ahead

Tip: Write these actions as reminders on the diary pages.

I commit to this goal wholeheartedly!

Sign here:

This Week

Use this week's Mercury/Saturn alignment to train your brain to look for the good in your life.

February 24: Mars retrograde ends

February 27: Dark Moon

February 27/28: New Moon occurs at 09°Pisces41'

March 2: Venus retrograde begins in Aries

Quote of the Week

'Change your thoughts and you change your world.'

Norman Vincent Peale

February–March – Week 9

24 Monday

♑

25 Tuesday

♑ ♒

26 Wednesday

♒

27 Thursday

New Moon: LA: 16:44 | New York: 19:44 ♒ ♓

28 Friday

New Moon: London: 00:44 | Sydney: 11:44 ♓

1 Saturday

♓ ♈

2 Sunday

♈

March

March 6/7: First Quarter Moon in Gemini

March 13/14: Full Moon eclipse in Virgo

March 22: Last Quarter Moon in Capricorn

March 29: Super New Moon eclipse in Aries

Watch out – it's an eclipse month! That means anything can happen and probably will. Moreover, we also have a major planetary shift taking place as Neptune, which rules dreams, soulmates, mysticism, and meditation, returns to Aries for the first time since 1875. Let's unpack this...

First off, the eclipses this month mean that life can turn in an instant, so don't be surprised if life at the start of March feels very different to life at the end of March. That's what eclipses are all about.

If you've been living life out of integrity or off the plan that you incarnated with, so to speak, eclipses are when you get back on track with the life your soul needs you to live to complete your dharma and karma. If you think all that sounds intense, you're right. Eclipses are intense – mainly because if you're resisting the inevitable in your life, eclipse seasons essentially ensure the inevitable finally happens. Are you ready?

In addition, Neptune is changing signs, so expect the energies this month to be anything from confusing to enlightening. Overall, it should be a month to remember. In the words of Rumi, 'Don't go back to sleep'!

And the planet of love and abundance, Venus, is starting one of her rare retrogrades. It can be a very good time to get back in touch with an ex and see how they're faring. Reconciliation or closure is on offer. If you've been waiting and waiting for some money to turn up, it may do during this cycle, which lasts about 40 nights.

This month I will:

- ❑ **Tie up the loose ends**
- ❑ **Make a new start**
- ❑ **Dream some new dreams**

This Week

Mercury meets Pluto this week, making it a good time to have a conversation that changes everything. Sort out as much as you can before the upcoming eclipses. Overall, positive energies are afoot.

March 3: Mercury into Aries

March 6/7: First Quarter Moon occurs at 16°Gemini21′

What Are You Grateful For This Week?

March – Week 10

3 Monday

♈♉

4 Tuesday

♉

5 Wednesday

♉♊

6 Thursday

First Quarter Moon ♊

7 Friday

First Quarter Moon ♊♋

8 Saturday

♋

9 Sunday

♋♌

Full Moon eclipse in Virgo

KEY WORDS AND IDEAS FOR THIS LUNATION:

- Too much too soon
- Too little too late
- Between a rock and a confusing place
- Old feelings coming up

DATE AND TIME OF THIS FULL MOON ECLIPSE

LA: Mar 13, 23:54 | New York: Mar 14, 02:54 | London: Mar 14, 06:54 | Sydney: Mar 14, 17:54

Looking at the chart for this Full Moon eclipse is like looking at a pileup of planets in something of a car crash. There are so many mixed energies that it's quite hard to express one cohesive, overall message for this Full Moon. The good news is that, ultimately, it promises change and that change promises to be rather positive.

With so many somewhat contradictory energies pulsating out of this eclipse, it's best to drill down to the basics.

An eclipse is when the Universe changes gears. If you haven't been living in accordance with what you need to do to fulfill your life purpose, this is when the Universe can thwack you right in the face so that you do. If you're already on the right path, then you really have nothing to worry about.

This is thanks to the aspects or alignments that this Full Moon is making to the planets. For example, it's harmoniously linking to the planet of change and liberation, Uranus. This suggests that some hard truths need to be faced if you want to move on from the past and align with what's best for your soul.

This is also a time to stop seeing someone or something through rose-tinted glasses and for dreams to become real, but there's a need to be realistic as well.

Note that as this Full Moon takes place just before Mercury goes retrograde on 15 March, it's a good time to tie up whatever loose ends you need to, to affect the changes you're seeking.

Do Something Radical!

Think about your life. Where do you feel trapped – even just a bit? Is there one routine or one habit or situation that you wish you could blow the lid off? If the answer is yes, then that's your homework for this week and this powerful Full Moon eclipse. Once you've identified what's holding you back, cut ties and set it free! Uranus is the planet of surprises and chaos, and sometimes when we do things like break free from something that's been holding us back, surprises and chaos follow. Try not to let that put you off. Ask yourself what your life would look like if you were free. Does it look preferable to now?

How to Work with This Moon

To discover where the energy of this Full Moon eclipse is for you, find your Star sign or Rising sign here, see which House is involved, and then read The Full Moon through the Houses (*see pages 16–19*): Aries – 6th House; Taurus – 5th House; Gemini – 4th House; Cancer – 3rd House; Leo – 2nd House; Virgo – 1st House; Libra – 12th House; Scorpio – 11th House; Sagittarius – 10th House; Capricorn – 9th House; Aquarius – 8th House; Pisces – 7th House.

FULL MOON FORGIVENESS AND QUESTIONS TO ASK

Eclipses bring with them powerful portals through which we can walk, should we decide to do so. It's very much a time when we can take the decision to change our life. That said, sometimes the change happens just because it's time. Good luck this week!

Am I ready to change my life, and if so, what's the number one thing in my life to change and why?

What steps do I need to take to make that change?

I wholeheartedly commit to taking the above steps and achieving this goal!

Sign here:

This Week

You can expect to feel the temperature soaring emotionally this week. This is because we're not just moving toward a Full Moon, but toward a Full Moon *eclipse*!

March 13/14: Full Moon eclipse occurs at 23°Virgo57'

March 15: Mercury goes retrograde in Aries

Quote of the Week

'You've been criticizing yourself for years and it hasn't worked. Try approving of yourself and see what happens.'

LOUISE HAY

March – Week 11

10 Monday

♌ ○

11 Tuesday

♌ ○

12 Wednesday

♌♍ ○

13 Thursday

Full Moon: LA: 23:54

♍ ○

14 Friday

Full Moon: New York: 02:54 | London: 06:54 | Sydney: 17:54

♍♎ ○

15 Saturday

♎ ○

16 Sunday

♎ ○

This Week

This week effectively marks the start of the new astrological year as the Sun moves back into the first sign of the zodiac, Aries. Forgive the past and move on now as we all begin again.

March 20: Sun into Aries;
Spring Equinox in the northern hemisphere (Ostara);
Autumn Equinox in the southern hemisphere (Mabon)

March 22: Last Quarter Moon occurs at 02°Capricorn05′

What Are You Grateful For This Week?

March – Week 12

17 Monday

♎ ♏ ○

18 Tuesday

♏ ○

19 Wednesday

♏ ♐ ◑

20 Thursday

♐ ◑

21 Friday

♐ ◑

22 Saturday

Last Quarter Moon ♐ ♑ ◑

23 Sunday

♑ ◑

Super New Moon eclipse in Aries

KEY WORDS AND IDEAS FOR THIS LUNATION:

- Start over
- Be brave
- Chase your dreams
- Get lucky

DATE AND TIME OF THIS SUPER NEW MOON ECLIPSE

LA: Mar 29, 03:57 | New York: Mar 29, 06:57 | London: Mar 29, 10:57 | Sydney: Mar 29, 21:57

Every now and then, the Universe really delivers. This New Moon is one of those times because it's taking place in the first sign of the Zodiac, Aries. At least once a year, we get a New Moon in Aries, offering us all a big chance for a new start. This New Moon isn't just a New Moon in Aries, it's also a Super New Moon eclipse ('Super' meaning that She is extra close to the Earth in Her orbit).

One of my favorite analogies for how to understand eclipses came from a US astrologer who was one of the few people to do in-depth work with the Moon and eclipses. Her name was Sophia Mason, and she put it like this:

> **'Let's say that at the New Moon, the energies are expressed in terms of you finding $10 you didn't know was in your jeans pocket. With the New Moon eclipse, you'll find $50.'**

This isn't literally a prediction that you're going to find money, though you might! It's about the fact that whatever happens now is supercharged. Even if you only make one set of New Moon wishes and set one lot of New Moon intentions all year, do it this New Moon. Make a 12-month plan – and don't delay! You have all the resources you need in the following pages.

The planet of communications, Mercury, is retrograde at the time of this New Moon eclipse. Moreover, it's retrograde in Aries, the same sign of the zodiac in which the eclipse is taking place. This means that whatever in your life is about to spring forward could also be connected to the past. Before too long, everything old could be new again.

Create a 12-Month Oracle Spread

The nature of this New Moon eclipse in the first sign of the zodiac, Aries, makes it the absolutely perfect time to create a 12-month plan. It would also help you to know about the energies you're likely to encounter as you carry out this plan.

Take a sheet of paper or your journal and draw up three rows of four columns to create a grid of 12 squares. Add the month names so that you've effectively created a little year-at-a-glance calendar. Now take a deck of oracle cards, shuffle, and draw one card for each month. Write the details of each card in the appropriate square of your grid.

As you carry out your 12-month plan, refer back to this card spread to see what energies are coming your way each month. It might only be the end of March/early April, but we're very much at the time of the astrological new year.

How to Work with This Moon

To discover where the energy of this Super New Moon eclipse is for you, find your Star sign or Rising sign here, see which House is involved, and then read The New Moon through the Houses (see *pages 12–15*): Aries – 1st House; Taurus – 12th House; Gemini – 11th House; Cancer – 10th House; Leo – 9th House; Virgo – 8th House; Libra – 7th House; Scorpio – 6th House; Sagittarius – 5th House; Capricorn – 4th House; Aquarius – 3rd House; Pisces – 2nd House.

NEW MOON WISHES AND INTENTIONS

My current biggest, most audacious goal, wish, or intention is:

Now turn it into an affirmation. Write it here as if it's already happened, and keep repeating it until the Full Moon.

Action steps I'm going to take toward this goal:

In the next 24 hours

In the coming week

In the month ahead

Tip: Write these actions as reminders on the diary pages.

I commit to this goal wholeheartedly!

Sign here:

This Week

This is very much the start of a new cycle with a New Moon eclipse in Aries; Venus and Mercury retrograding from Aries back into Pisces; and Neptune moving into Aries.

March 24: St. Gabriel's feast day

March 27: Venus retrogrades back into Pisces

March 28: Dark Moon

March 29: Super New Moon eclipse occurs at 09°Aries00′

March 30: Mercury retrogrades back into Pisces; Neptune into Aries

Quote of the Week

'Whatever you can do, or dream you can do, begin it. Boldness has genius, power, and magic in it. Begin it now.'

JOHANN WOLFGANG VON GOETHE

March – Week 13

24 Monday

♑ ♒

25 Tuesday

♒

26 Wednesday

♒ ♓

27 Thursday

♓

28 Friday

♓ ♈

29 Saturday

New Moon: LA: 03:57 | New York: 06:57 | London: 10:57 | Sydney: 21:57 ♈

30 Sunday

♈ ♉

April

April 4/5: First Quarter Moon in Cancer

April 12/13: Full Moon in Libra

April 20/21: Last Quarter Moon in Aquarius

April 27/28: Super New Moon in Taurus

April should start to feel like it's making a lot more sense. What felt unclear in recent weeks and months should start to reveal itself. Where you were unsure, you'll start to feel like you have the information you need to move forward. If you've been using this diary to its potential, where you've been rethinking and reevaluating situations in your life, you should now have some 'findings' that will inform your next steps.

We really have been through a bit of a portal of change in the past few months. We've had the eclipses, both Mercury and Venus retrograding, and Neptune has changed signs, which is massive. Now we're more or less in the aftermath of all that.

This month sees Mercury retrograde ending on April 7 and Venus retrograde ending on April 13. In what's a relatively rare occurrence, we'll have all the planets moving forward for once. Plus we have a major alignment between Saturn and Uranus – all your hard work can pay off now.

The main thing is to try to move past any regrets and focus on what you want. While it's sometimes tempting to nurse your pain and keep going over what you've lost, it's far more productive to forgive the past and start over, especially now, with the energies being so forward-moving.

Even if you're hoping for life to go back to what it once was, come into the present and create the right environment for that to happen.

This month I will:

- ❑ **Act on the info I have now**
- ❑ **Make seismic life changes**
- ❑ **Learn to love again**

This Week

This is a potentially amazing week thanks to a powerful and rare Saturn alignment with Uranus. If you work hard and make a big effort, positive changes could be the result sooner rather than later.

April 4: Saturn harmonizes with Uranus

April 4/5: First Quarter Moon occurs at 15°Cancer33′

What Are You Grateful For This Week?

March – April – Week 14

31 Monday

♉

1 Tuesday

♉♊

2 Wednesday

♊

3 Thursday

♊♋

4 Friday

First Quarter Moon ♋

5 Saturday

First Quarter Moon ♋

6 Sunday

♋♌

Full Moon in Libra

KEY WORDS AND IDEAS FOR THIS LUNATION:

- Relationships in focus
- Reevaluate your love life
- Don't argue
- Avoid power struggles

DATE AND TIME OF THIS FULL MOON

LA: Apr 12, 17:22 | **New York:** Apr 12, 20:22 | **London:** Apr 13, 01:22 | **Sydney:** Apr 13, 10:22

At least once a year, the Universe is thoughtful enough to send us a Full Moon in the sign of Libra. Why is this thoughtful? Because the Full Moon is all about letting go of drama and upsets, and Libra is the relationship sign. So, once a year, around this time, we get a chance to let go of relationship drama and move on.

If you're single, maybe you're still hurting from something that happened to you in the past. If you're attached, perhaps there are issues between you and your beloved that you need to work through. Or it could be that you and your partner are ready to go to the next level, which is also very possible when the Full Moon is in the relationship sign of Libra.

This Full Moon is clashing with Mars and Pluto, which does not make a very harmonious relationship. Tread carefully in a relationship, personal or professional, that's already shaky and perhaps verging on angry.

Additionally, Venus retrograde ends the same day as the Full Moon lights up the skies. By now you should have worked out what really matters to you. Now you just need to think about how to prioritize your objectives. You'll be amazed at how hard it is for people to do this sometimes.

Overall, this is a pretty intense Full Moon in Libra. It's definitely possible to use it to move on from relationship upsets; however, you need to make sure you do it in as calm and healthy a way possible. If someone around you is acting in a toxic manner, avoid getting drawn into their drama.

A Post-Venus Retrograde Exercise

Think back to 2 March when the most recent Venus retrograde cycle began. I hope you've got the message by now that this has been a time to reevaluate everything in your life, to weigh what really matters, and to take action based on those findings. Look back at the list you made for the 'What Really Matters?' exercise (see *page 64*). Have you been living your life in accordance with those things? If not, can you see what threw you off track? Use the Libra Full Moon to release anything hampering you.

How to Work with This Moon

To discover where the energy of this Full Moon is for you, find your Star sign or Rising sign here, see which House is involved, and then read The Full Moon through the Houses (see *pages 16–19*): Aries – 7th House; Taurus – 6th House; Gemini – 5th House; Cancer – 4th House; Leo – 3rd House; Virgo – 2nd House; Libra – 1st House; Scorpio – 12th House; Sagittarius – 11th House; Capricorn – 10th House; Aquarius – 9th House; Pisces – 8th House.

FULL MOON FORGIVENESS AND QUESTIONS TO ASK

This is a slightly angry Full Moon, so it's time to turn inward a little and think about how you've been expressing your disagreements and disappointments, etc. Have you been letting them rip? Too much? Too little? Or have you been bottling them up? If so, go easy now, as they could all come pouring out too easily.

What is your relationship with confrontation like? Understanding this will help you understand yourself in relationships.

Would you say you're an anxious, avoidant, or secure type in relationships, and how does that inform how you behave?

If you've been losing your temper lately, how can you keep your cool? Or is your anger empowering you at the moment?

This Week

It's a Full Moon week, and the latest Mercury *and* Venus retrogrades are ending. Therefore, life could look quite different at the end of the week than it did at the beginning!

April 7: Mercury retrograde ends

April 12/13: Full Moon occurs at 23° Libra 20′

April 13: Venus retrograde ends

Quote of the Week

'We all make mistakes. How we correct them is what makes all the difference between success and failure.'

Zane Baker, meditation teacher

April – Week 15

7 Monday

♌ ◐

8 Tuesday

♌♍ ◐

9 Wednesday

♍ ○

10 Thursday

♍ ○

11 Friday

♍♎ ○

12 Saturday

Full Moon: LA: 17:22 | New York: 20:22 ♎ ○

13 Sunday

Full Moon: London: 01:22 | Sydney: 10:22 ♎♏ ○

This Week

Mercury moves into Aries this week, and Mars moves into Leo. That's a whole lot of very fiery power we're all now dealing with. You have been warned! Watch out for flaring tempers.

April 16: Mercury into Aries

April 18: Mars into Leo

April 19: Sun into Taurus

April 20/21: Last Quarter Moon occurs at 01°Aquarius12'

What Are You Grateful For This Week?

April – Week 16

14 Monday

♏ ○

15 Tuesday

♏ ○

16 Wednesday

♏ ♐ ○

17 Thursday

♐ ○

18 Friday

♐ ♑ ○

19 Saturday

♑ ○

20 Sunday

Last Quarter Moon ♑ ♒ ◑

Super New Moon in Taurus

KEY WORDS AND IDEAS FOR THIS LUNATION:

- Tense
- Sexy
- Dreamy
- Healing

DATE AND TIME OF THIS SUPER NEW MOON

LA: Apr 27, 12:31 | New York: Apr 27, 15:31 | London: Apr 27, 20:31 | Sydney: Apr 28, 05:31

There's quite a lot of pressure building at the time of this Super New Moon. It's creating what's called a T-Square in disguise with angry Mars and furious Pluto. This is like the stars spelling out the word T-E-N-S-I-O-N!

This energy has been building for a while. You may recall that the previous Full Moon was also caught in the middle of a Mars/Pluto argument, and that's something not to be underestimated!

Anger could flare all too easily at this New Moon, so if you're walking on eggshells around someone or a situation, take extra care. After all, Mars is the angry planet and Pluto is the furious one!

To have an idea of where in your life this tension is likely to play out, look at the How to Work with This Moon section on the following page. Read up on the part of your life being triggered, as that's where you can expect a lot of intensity!

That said, Mars and Pluto do both have their sexy side, so there could be a bit of that in the air under this New Moon – if you want a more sexy existence, make sure you include that in your New Moon wishes. I'd say more, but there's a slightly vulgar side to this alignment, and I don't want to offend anyone, so please use your imagination. Suffice to say, #darkside. ☺

There's also a super-dreamy and possibly even a romantic side to this New Moon, as the lunation's ruler, Venus, is aligning with the planet of dreams, soulmates, and poetry, Neptune, just a few days later.

What Would It Look Like If It Were Healed?

In the nineties, I traveled to the Swiss Alps to do an amazing chakra healing course with the late, great Martin Brofman. He taught us to visualize people seeking healing as already healed and to hold that thought in our heads. What would they look like if they were healed? What would it look like if you were healed in whatever part of your life that needs healing? (Most of us have something we need to heal.) Ask yourself what your *life* would look like if that thing were healed... and then focus on healing. The easiest way heal is to practice Full Moon forgiveness, but even at the New Moon, you can set intentions that support your desire to heal.

How to Work with This Moon

To discover where the energy of this Super New Moon is for you, find your Star sign or Rising sign here, see which House is involved, and then read The New Moon through the Houses (see *pages 12–15*): Aries – 2nd House; Taurus – 1st House; Gemini – 12th House; Cancer – 11th House; Leo – 10th House; Virgo – 9th House; Libra – 8th House; Scorpio – 7th House; Sagittarius – 6th House; Capricorn – 5th House; Aquarius – 4th House; Pisces – 3rd House.

NEW MOON WISHES AND INTENTIONS

My current biggest, most audacious goal, wish, or intention is:

Now turn it into an affirmation. Write it here as if it's already happened, and keep repeating it until the Full Moon.

Action steps I'm going to take toward this goal:

In the next 24 hours

In the coming week

In the month ahead

Tip: Write these actions as reminders on the diary pages.

I commit to this goal wholeheartedly!

Sign here:

This Week

It may not be the jolliest time of the year, thanks to the current alignments, but there's still a lot of spiritual work to be done. What lessons are you learning from life right now? That's probably the most important question.

April 20/21: Last Quarter Moon occurs at 01°Aquarius12'

April 26: Dark Moon

April 27/28: Super New Moon occurs at 07°Taurus47'

What Are You Grateful For This Week?

____

____

____

____

April – Week 17

21 Monday

Last Quarter Moon ♒

22 Tuesday

♒

23 Wednesday

♒ ♓

24 Thursday

♓

25 Friday

♓ ♈

26 Saturday

♈

27 Sunday

New Moon: LA: 12:31 | New York: 15:31 | London: 20:31 ♈ ♉

May

May 4: First Quarter Moon in Leo

May 12/13: Full Moon in Scorpio

May 20: Last Quarter Moon in Aquarius

May 26/27: New Moon in Gemini

There's really only one thing to lead with this month, and it's the momentous move of seriously important Saturn. Having spent the past couple of years in Pisces, Saturn is moving into the first sign of the zodiac, Aries. This is important astrologically on so many levels:

1. Saturn only changes signs every two or so years.
2. Saturn is the Lord of Karma.
3. Where Saturn goes, lessons follow.
4. Aries is the first sign of the zodiac, so Saturn's move here is the start of a new cycle for the world.
5. To know where this is happening in your chart, check which House the New Moon in Aries is triggering for you (*see page 82*).

Note that Saturn will only be in Aries from May 25 to September 1 because, as so often happens when an outer planet changes signs, Saturn will retrograde back into Pisces where it's been on and off since 2023.

It's very much a month to live consciously. That means being aware of what's going on around you and doing your Full Moon release work and setting your New Moon intentions. Otherwise, this Saturn stuff can come up and bite you on the butt!

To help with this Moon work, I've recorded a chant for you, which you can find in the Diary Bonuses Area of my site (*see page 22*).

This month I will:

- ❑ **Learn my lessons**
- ❑ **Be realistic**
- ❑ **Find out where Saturn is for me now**

This Week

This could be the most romantic week you've had in a long time – unless you're with someone shady you can't trust, in which case, ask yourself why you're with them.

April 30: Venus into Aries

April 30/May 1: Beltane in the northern hemisphere (May Day); Samhain in the southern hemisphere

May 4: May the 4th be with you; First Quarter Moon occurs at 14°Leo21′; Pluto goes retrograde in Aquarius

What Are You Grateful For This Week?

April–May – Week 18

28 Monday

New Moon: Sydney: 05:31 ♉ 🌑

---

29 Tuesday

♉♊ 🌒

---

30 Wednesday

♊ 🌒

---

1 Thursday

♊♋ 🌒

---

2 Friday

♋ 🌒

---

3 Saturday

♋♌ 🌒

---

4 Sunday

First Quarter Moon ♌ 🌓

This Week

There's a lot of positivity in the skies this week, with some lovely alignments between communications planet Mercury, lucky Jupiter, and loving Venus. Make the most of it by having as good a time as you can!

May 10: Mercury moves into Taurus

What Are You Grateful For This Week?

May – Week 19

5 Monday

♌ ♍ ◐

6 Tuesday

♍ ◐

7 Wednesday

♍ ◐

8 Thursday

♍ ♎ ◐

9 Friday

♎ ○

10 Saturday

♎ ♏ ○

11 Sunday

♏ ○

Full Moon in Scorpio

KEY WORDS AND IDEAS FOR THIS LUNATION:

- Let go of a grudge
- Drop the drama
- Surprise someone
- Surprise yourself

DATE AND TIME OF THIS FULL MOON

LA: May 12, 09:55 | New York: May 12, 12:55 | London: May 12, 17:55 | Sydney: May 13, 02:55

Somewhat unfortunately, there's a rather harsh link between the planet of communications, Mercury, and the planet of paranoia, Pluto. If you're feeling overwhelmed around the time of this Full Moon, try to give yourself a break. Sometimes it's just a matter of not indulging yourself when you start feeling sad about something; sometimes it's about forgiving someone even though you feel really angry; and sometimes it's just about focusing on the here and now so you don't let the wheels of your mind drive you crazy.

Full Moons are always intense, but this one could be extra intense because of the Mercury–Pluto alignment.

That said, Pluto is also the detox planet, and Mercury is the planet of the mind, so if you need to detox your mind, this is the perfect time to do so. There's an exercise on the following page to help you.

The good news is that there's also a lot of healing in the air under this Full Moon, if you're willing to tap into it. It could be a good time for what's known as a 'healing crisis' – one that can be hard to deal with initially but ultimately proves healing.

The massive planet Jupiter that knows how to look on the bright side is headed toward a harmonious link with the wounded planetoid Chiron. One thing to remember now, whatever you're going through, is that sometimes it just takes a firm decision to kick off the healing process.

If you go into this Full Moon wanting to make amends with someone (or even wanting to purge them from your life!), you should be able to get the best that this lunation has to offer.

The Mirror Technique

One of the first steps toward detoxing our minds is recognizing that the people who trigger us are often only a reflection of a part of ourselves that we don't like. In other words, if you're triggered by someone who is ungenerous with their money, for example, think about your own attitude toward money. Think about the person who triggers you most and write down their three or five worst habits. What you don't like in them is what you need to address in yourself. This is a very confronting exercise, but perfect to do at the time of the deep and dark Scorpio Full Moon with the Mercury/Pluto clash.

How to Work with This Moon

To discover where the energy of this Full Moon is for you, find your Star sign or Rising sign here, see which House is involved, and then read The Full Moon through the Houses (see *pages 16–19*): Aries – 8th House; Taurus – 7th House; Gemini – 6th House; Cancer – 5th House; Leo – 4th House; Virgo – 3rd House; Libra – 2nd House; Scorpio – 1st House; Sagittarius – 12th House; Capricorn – 11th House; Aquarius – 10th House; Pisces – 9th House.

FULL MOON FORGIVENESS AND QUESTIONS TO ASK

Journaling about your feelings is one of the best ways to do shadow work, detox yourself mentally, and work through hard feelings. The monthly Full Moon questions in this diary are designed to prompt you to go within. Do them in extra depth this month and use extra paper if needed.

What triggers you the most?

____

____

____

What unhealed experience is causing you to be triggered?

____

____

____

Can you forgive this trauma, and what would your life look like if you did?

____

____

____

This Week

There's always healing in the air. Is it possible to refuse to be healed? For sure! So are you refusing to be healed? If not, breathe in, because there are healing vibes in the air this Full Moon week.

May 12/13: Full Moon occurs at 22°Scorpio13'

May 18: Jupiter harmonizes with Chiron

Quote of the Week

'Anything can be healed.'

Martin Brofman

May – Week 20

12 Monday

Full Moon: LA: 09:55 | New York: 12:55 | London: 17:55 ♏→○

13 Tuesday

Full Moon: Sydney: 02:55 ♏→♐○

14 Wednesday

♐○

15 Thursday

♐♑○

16 Friday

♑○

17 Saturday

♑◐

18 Sunday

♑♒◐

This Week

It's a red-letter week astrologically as the planet of karma, Saturn, changes signs, moving from Pisces into Aries. Saturn hasn't been in Aries since 1999.

May 20: Last Quarter Moon occurs at 29°Aquarius43'; Sun into Gemini

May 25: Saturn into Aries

What Are You Grateful For This Week?

May – Week 21

19 Monday

♒

20 Tuesday

Last Quarter Moon ♒♓

21 Wednesday

♓

22 Thursday

♓♈

23 Friday

♈

24 Saturday

♈♉

25 Sunday

♉

New Moon in Gemini

KEY WORDS AND IDEAS FOR THIS LUNATION:

- Right a wrong
- Congratulate yourself
- Take action
- Express yourself

DATE AND TIME OF THIS NEW MOON

LA: May 26, 20:02 | New York: May 26, 23:02 | London: May 27, 04:02 | Sydney: May 27, 13:02

One thing you quickly learn when you start to work with astrology is this: life really does go in cycles. That's because the planets are moving around the Sun and repeating or echoing or triggering one another and their patterns. May's Full Moon in Scorpio, for example, clashed with Pluto, which brought intense energies and undoubtedly caused headaches for a lot of people. Luckily, this New Moon is very different!

Mercury has kept moving forward since May, and under this New Moon is going to be harmonizing with Pluto.

This New Moon brings a chance to right a wrong, to say the thing you meant to but didn't because you were too angry at the time, or to clear your head now that the mental toxicity has been cleared out.

Additionally, this New Moon is in Gemini, the sign that's all about mental processes, communications, and everything else that Mercury covers. So if you need to kiss and make up with someone, make that one of your intentions under the New Moon.

One thing life has taught me is that communication is everything in relationships. This New Moon is not to a time to stay quiet. Set an intention to express yourself. If you talk things through now, you could end up nipping some major issues in the bud before they escalate and it's too late.

This New Moon is very positive overall and also aligns harmoniously with Venus and Mars, so it augurs well for romance. If you go into it expecting good things, you just might get them!

Take an Inventory

With the energies so positive this month, it's tempting to just recommend you enjoy them. However, this diary is all about helping you to live your best life, so how about we flip that around and say the energies are so positive that it's a good time to do a little bit of hard work on your life path? Take a full and honest inventory of anyone you've hurt, either recently or in the past, and consider getting in touch with them to ask for their forgiveness and make amends. The only exception to this would be if it means reopening a wound that's since healed.

How to Work with This Moon

To discover where the energy of this New Moon is for you, find your Star sign or Rising sign here, see which House is involved, and then read The New Moon through the Houses (*see pages 12–15*): Aries – 3rd House; Taurus – 2nd House; Gemini – 1st House; Cancer – 12th House; Leo – 11th House; Virgo – 10th House; Libra – 9th House; Scorpio – 8th House; Sagittarius – 7th House; Capricorn – 6th House; Aquarius – 5th House; Pisces – 4th House.

NEW MOON WISHES AND INTENTIONS

My current biggest, most audacious goal, wish, or intention is:

Now turn it into an affirmation. Write it here as if it's already happened, and keep repeating it until the Full Moon.

Action steps I'm going to take toward this goal:

In the next 24 hours

In the coming week

In the month ahead

Tip: Write these actions as reminders on the diary pages.

I commit to this goal wholeheartedly!

Sign here:

This Week

The New Moon takes place in communication sign of Gemini and is aligned with communication planet Mercury. This is astrology doublespeak for 'If you don't express yourself now, you may never!'

May 26: Mercury into Gemini; Dark Moon

May 26/27: New Moon occurs at 06°Gemini06'

Quote of the Week

'As I allow myself the space to watch without judgment and without criticism, I begin to make great progress in loving communication.'

Louise Hay

May–June – Week 22

26 Monday

New Moon: LA: 20:02 | New York: 23:02

♉♊

27 Tuesday

New Moon: London: 04:02 | Sydney: 13:02

♊

28 Wednesday

♊♋

29 Thursday

♋

30 Friday

♋♌

31 Saturday

♌

1 Sunday

♌

June

June 2/3: First Quarter Moon in Virgo

June 11: Full Moon in Sagittarius

June 18/19: Last Quarter Moon in Pisces

June 25: New Moon in Cancer

Some months just have extra power, and this is one of them. Hot on the heels of Saturn changing signs last month, this month we have the planet of plenty, Jupiter, doing the same thing. This means that we're starting to get into a very different landscape astrologically, so don't be surprised if your life feels like it's changing.

Sometimes we're just cruising along and taking everything for granted, and then these big planets start changing the way they've been doing things lately, and we get wake-up calls and suddenly realize that we need to pay a little bit more attention to what's going on in our life.

So use this month to count your blessings and realize what you've got so you're less likely to mess around and lose it. Plus, Jupiter, which is so active this month, is all about appreciation and gratitude and the blessings that being in that state brings.

I've trotted this phrase out many times, but it's so true that I'm going to do it again now: as Oprah Winfrey said, the more we praise and celebrate our lives, the more we have to praise and celebrate. In particular, this month, Jupiter is moving into the home and family sign of Cancer, so if you're trying to have a happier personal life, Jupiter is there to help.

More importantly, though, have a look at the New Moon in Cancer and see which house is being triggered for you (see *page 138*). The same part of your chart is getting extra blessings and good luck from Jupiter's move this week.

This month I will:

- ❑ **Count my blessings**
- ❑ **Make up with family**
- ❑ **Believe in my own good luck**

This Week

There's romance in the air this week, so compliment your beloved, if you have one, or get out there and send a little wink to someone you like the look of. This week is also very good for conversations around money.

June 2/3: First Quarter Moon occurs at 12°Virgo50'

June 6: Venus into Taurus

June 8: Mercury into Cancer

What Are You Grateful For This Week?

June – Week 23

2 Monday

First Quarter Moon ♌ ♍ ◐

3 Tuesday

First Quarter Moon ♍ ◐

4 Wednesday

♍ ♎ ◐

5 Thursday

♎ ◐

6 Friday

♎ ◐

7 Saturday

♎ ♏ ○

8 Sunday

♏ ○

Full Moon in Sagittarius

KEY WORDS AND IDEAS FOR THIS LUNATION:

- Say something kind
- Don't fight what is
- Decide to heal
- See the funny side

DATE AND TIME OF THIS FULL MOON

LA: Jun 11, 00:43 | New York: Jun 11, 03:43 | London: Jun 11, 08:43 | Sydney: Jun 11, 17:43

Full Moons are always intense, and this one is probably going to be no exception, particularly as it's clashing with the karmic lunar nodes. The way to get ahead of any potentially aggravating energies is to be as kind as you can, regardless of who you're dealing with. In a world that often feels tumultuous and overwhelming, a few well-placed kind words can go a very long way.

This Full Moon takes place just ahead of a lovely Mercury/Venus alignment, so tune in to the power of being thoughtful.

That said, there are some slightly challenging energies around now. We all know that life can be unpredictable, and this Full Moon could bring around some situations where we just want to rail against what is. As much as I strongly believe in the law of attraction and holding the vision of life as you want it to be, there are times when we also have to accept what is and move on from there. If you're in a situation right now that feels extremely stuck, open your eyes to it as this Full Moon unfolds and ask the Universe to help show you the way.

Since this Full Moon is taking place in the comedy sign of Sagittarius, finding your sense of humor, if it's been lost lately, will be really useful. It'll help you navigate any challenges coming up now.

Note that the more you can release any pent-up dramas under the Full Moon, the less reactive you will be in the days that follow. Also that the further out we get from this Full Moon, the stranger life could become. Whatever you're going through now, decide that you want to heal and the healing process will begin. It really can be that simple if you allow it.

Create a Gratitude Jar

This exercise requires a little bit of extra effort, but I promise you'll find it's worth it. It's simple: Find the largest glass jar you can with a lid. Every day, make it a practice to rip off a small piece of paper and write down something good that happened that day, something that you're grateful for, or something that made you happy. Before too long, you'll have a jar full of happy memories that you can draw on whenever you're feeling a bit down in the dumps.

How to Work with This Moon

To discover where the energy of this Full Moon is for you, find your Star sign or Rising sign here, see which House is involved, and then read The Full Moon through the Houses (*see pages 16–19*): Aries – 9th House; Taurus – 8th House; Gemini – 7th House; Cancer – 6th House; Leo – 5th House; Virgo – 4th House; Libra – 3rd House; Scorpio – 2nd House; Sagittarius – 1st House; Capricorn – 12th House; Aquarius – 11th House; Pisces – 10th House.

FULL MOON FORGIVENESS AND QUESTIONS TO ASK

This week, speak kindly, accept reality, choose healing, and laugh, and it could turn out to be a very positive Full Moon. That said, it's still a good time to access your emotions, so use these prompts to inspire a little journaling.

Is there someone you haven't been terribly nice to lately, and what would your relationship look like if you started speaking to them in a kinder fashion?

Where in your life have you got rose-tinted glasses on that are so thick that you're not seeing things clearly? What does accepting this mean for your next action?

Who's the funniest person you know, and how hard would it be for you to message them to suggest a meetup this week? Are you willing to do it?

This Week

Jupiter moves into Cancer this week, then clashes with Saturn – so it's going to be a week of swings and roundabouts. Don't let anyone rain on your parade.

June 9: Jupiter into Cancer

June 11: Full Moon occurs at 20°Sagittarius39′

June 15: Jupiter clashes with Saturn

Quote of the Week

'Always look on the bright side of life.'

Monty Python

June – Week 24

9 Monday

♏→♐

10 Tuesday

♐

11 Wednesday

Full Moon: LA: 00:43 | New York: 03:43 | London: 08:43 | Sydney: 17:43 ♐

12 Thursday

♐♑

13 Friday

♑

14 Saturday

♑♒

15 Sunday

♒

This Week

Hot off a confrontation with Saturn, Jupiter now clashes with Neptune. Expect lots of inspiration and meditation, but also deception and disappointment!

June 17: Mars into Virgo

June 18/19: Last Quarter Moon occurs at 27°Pisces47′

June 19: Jupiter clashes with Neptune

June 21: Sun into Cancer;
Winter Solstice in the southern hemisphere (Yule);
Summer Solstice in the northern hemisphere (Litha)

What Are You Grateful For This Week?

June – Week 25

16 Monday

♒♓

---

17 Tuesday

♓

---

18 Wednesday

Last Quarter Moon ♓♈

---

19 Thursday

Last Quarter Moon ♈

---

20 Friday

♈

---

21 Saturday

♈♉

---

22 Sunday

♉

New Moon in Cancer

KEY WORDS AND IDEAS FOR THIS LUNATION:

- Work on your dreams
- Nurture yourself
- Adore your family
- Get lucky (again!)

DATE AND TIME OF THIS NEW MOON

LA: Jun 25, 03:31 | New York: Jun 25, 06:31 | London: Jun 25, 11:31 | Sydney: Jun 25, 20:31

The first thing to know about this New Moon is that it's very much a time to be your most dynamic self. People think of Cancer as a sign that's all about staying at home and baking cakes, but it's also one of the Cardinal signs (along with Aries, Libra, and Capricorn) that begin at the equinoxes and Solstices, and mark the beginning of the seasons. Basically, it means it's a very powerful sign.

The New Moon in Cancer is always a very good time to bring out your most dynamic self... and maybe spend some time with your beloved family.

This New Moon speaks of good news coming quickly, changes that you've been hoping to make, the wheels of life being greased, easier conversations, and mental fluidity. What more could we want?

Add in a little cake-baking and -eating, and it's all beginning to sound pretty great!

An important note about this New Moon is that it's making a harmonious connection to the planet of drive and determination, Mars. In other words, this is New Moon has a ton of get-up-and-go, so make your wishes and act on them!

This New Moon also sees a fantastic Mercury/Uranus alignment taking place just afterward. Overall, communications are particularly well starred, so make sure you reach out to someone if you've been finding it difficult to talk to them lately. It's actually a very good time for manifesting as well, as Mercury triggers both of the leading manifestation planets, Saturn and Neptune.

Focus on Manifesting

Saturn meeting Neptune can have a tough expression, but we're focusing on manifesting the best of the best here! This week, spend a little time every day observing *what* you're thinking about. Are you focusing on the positive or are you focusing on the negative? This can apply in a relationship as much as a job or a situation of any kind. If you only focus on the negative, you're just going to get more negative. It's the law of attraction. It's also the secret of New Moon manifesting. Once you understand this, you basically have the keys to the Universe!

How to Work with This Moon

To discover where the energy of this New Moon is for you, find your Star sign or Rising sign here, see which House is involved, and then read The New Moon through the Houses (see *pages 12–15*): Aries – 4th House; Taurus – 3rd House; Gemini – 2nd House; Cancer – 1st House; Leo – 12th House; Virgo – 11th House; Libra – 10th House; Scorpio – 9th House; Sagittarius – 8th House; Capricorn – 7th House; Aquarius – 6th House; Pisces – 5th House.

NEW MOON WISHES AND INTENTIONS

My current biggest, most audacious goal, wish, or intention is:

Now turn it into an affirmation. Write it here as if it's already happened, and keep repeating it until the Full Moon.

Action steps I'm going to take toward this goal:

In the next 24 hours

In the coming week

In the month ahead

Tip: Write these actions as reminders on the diary pages.

I commit to this goal wholeheartedly!

Sign here:

This Week

The New Moon this week is a good one – make sure you get yourself into the most positive frame of mind that you can muster; that's the way to start New Moon manifesting really well!

June 24: Dark Moon

June 25: New Moon occurs at 04°Cancer08′

June 26: Mercury into Leo

Quote of the Week

'Luck is believing you're lucky.'

TENNESSEE WILLIAMS

June – Week 26

23 Monday

♉♊

24 Tuesday

♊

25 Wednesday

New Moon: LA: 03:31 | New York: 06:31 | London: 11:31 | Sydney: 20:31 ♊♋

26 Thursday

♋

27 Friday

♋♌

28 Saturday

♌

29 Sunday

♌♍

July

July 2/3: First Quarter Moon in Libra

July 10/11: Full Moon in Capricorn

July 17/18: Last Quarter Moon in Aries

July 24/25: New Moon in Leo

Back in May I said that Saturn was changing signs, and last month I mentioned that Jupiter was changing signs, both of which would change the astrological landscape. Well, don't breathe out just yet, because this month sees outer planet Uranus changing signs.

The fact that Uranus is an outer planet gives greater importance to the move. Uranus will leave Taurus (where it's been since 2018) and take up residence in Gemini until November when it'll retrograde back into Taurus until next year.

You need to know that Uranus is the disruptor planet. It's the planet of liberation and awakenings and electricity and chaos. Wherever it goes, all of that follows!

To find out which part of your chart is being triggered by Uranus, check which house is being activated by the New Moon in Gemini (see *How to Work with This Moon, page 120*). Make sure you look at your Rising sign for more accurate results. If you don't know your Rising sign, you can find it out for free at my site (see *page 22*). And the prediction? Wherever in your life Uranus goes, upheaval follows. That might sound ominous, but it's quite often the upheaval we had to have!

The other major news this month is that Neptune, Saturn, and Chiron are all going retrograde on July 4, 13, and 30, respectively. So prepare to turn a little more inward. Why? Because retrogrades are always about the energy of the planet turning in on itself, plus you get second chances in the part of your life being triggered.

This month I will:

- ❑ **Get back to meditation**
- ❑ **Live and let live**
- ❑ **Wake TF up!**

This Week

Romances could take a sudden turn for the better this week as loving Venus connects with surprising Uranus, committed Saturn, and dreamy Neptune. It's a case of taking steps to make your dreams real.

July 2/3: First Quarter Moon occurs at 11°Libra09′

July 4: Venus into Gemini; Neptune retrograde begins

What Are You Grateful For This Week?

June–July – Week 27

30 Monday

♍

1 Tuesday

♍ ♎

2 Wednesday

First Quarter Moon ♎

3 Thursday

First Quarter Moon ♎

4 Friday

♎ ♏

5 Saturday

♏

6 Sunday

♏ ♐

Full Moon in Capricorn

KEY WORDS AND IDEAS FOR THIS LUNATION:

- Work–life balance
- Structure needed
- Romance settles down (post Venus/Uranus)
- Knowledge is power

DATE AND TIME OF THIS FULL MOON

LA: Jul 10, 13:36 | New York: Jul 10, 16:36 | London: Jul 10, 21:36 | Sydney: Jul 11, 06:36

To understand this lunation, we need to strip it back to basics. Work with it by first thinking about how ambitious (or not) you've been lately. Have you been working too hard and neglecting your personal life? Or vice versa? A rebalancing of this situation is called for. Have you been ruthless? Sometimes we feel like we need to be – but do we really? Is that not just an outdated, patriarchal paradigm that we can drop? Think about whether you can work smarter, rather than harder.

Another question to ponder this lunation is: *Where in your life have you been allowing your head to rule your heart?* Capricorn is all about logic and facts. It's the energy you use playing chess and working out, three moves ahead, how to take your opponent's queen. But the Full Moon in Capricorn can only happen when the Sun is in Cancer, which is the sign of home and family and soft underbellies.

At this Full Moon, ask yourself whether you've been too hard-hearted, or hardheaded, and if the answer is 'yes,' think about how that has served you.

It's so easy to fall into the trap of thinking that to be successful, we have to crush our rivals or competitors, and that we need to hustle to get anywhere and be available 24/7. This Full Moon reminds us that there is more to life than work.

It's also a time to be honest about whether you've been trying too hard to control someone else too. No one likes to be controlled (unless they have some kind of domination fantasy!).

Plan Ahead

The Full Moon in Capricorn is wonderful to use as a kind of midyear marker to work out where you are with your ambitions for 2025. One of the best ways to do this is to grab a deck of oracle cards or tarot cards, give them a good shuffle, and choose six to represent the months July through to December. You can lay them in two lines of three cards, or a circle of all six cards. Be sure to remember which card represents which month. Deal them out face down, slowly turn them over, and make notes in your journal to create a kind of prediction about what lies ahead in each month for you.

How to Work with This Moon

To discover where the energy of this Full Moon is for you, find your Star sign or Rising sign here, see which House is involved, and then read The Full Moon through the Houses (see *pages 16–19*): Aries – 10th House; Taurus – 9th House; Gemini – 8th House; Cancer – 7th House; Leo – 6th House; Virgo – 5th House; Libra – 4th House; Scorpio – 3rd House; Sagittarius – 2nd House; Capricorn – 1st House; Aquarius – 12th House; Pisces – 11th House.

FULL MOON FORGIVENESS AND QUESTIONS TO ASK

This is a super-powerful time energetically. If you're feeling stuck, think about the reasons why you haven't moved on from the past. Do you feel ready to surrender any tension and find release?

If you were to be kinder to yourself, what would that look like?

Is there someone you need to say sorry to, and are you willing to say it? Write a little bit about that situation.

Name one person at work who you're going to try harder to get along with within the next month. Think of one thing you can do as a starting point.

This Week

This week sees the hugely important move of the planet of chaos and madness, Uranus, into the sign of Gemini. It definitely augurs well for more technology, but watch out for people saying things that are just designed to shock you.

July 7: Uranus into Gemini

July 10/11: Full Moon occurs at 18°Capricorn50′

July 13: Saturn goes retrograde

Quote of the Week

'Life doesn't owe us anything. We only owe ourselves, to make the most of the life we are living, of the time we have left, and to live in gratitude.'

BRONNIE WARE, *THE TOP FIVE REGRETS OF THE DYING*

July – Week 28

7 Monday

♐ ○

8 Tuesday

♐ ○

9 Wednesday

♐ ♑ ○

10 Thursday

Full Moon: LA: 13:36 | New York: 16:36 | London: 21:36 ♑ ○

11 Friday

Full Moon: Sydney: 06:36 ♑ ♒ ○

12 Saturday

♒ ○

13 Sunday

♒ ♓ ○

This Week

Mercury, the planet of communication, starts 'going backward' in the skies this week and pretty soon manages a clash with Venus. Don't be surprised if you're feeling confused about love or money but you don't know why.

July 17/18: Last Quarter Moon occurs at 25°Aries40'

July 18: Mercury goes retrograde in Leo

What Are You Grateful For This Week?

July – Week 29

14 Monday

♓ ○

15 Tuesday

♓ ○

16 Wednesday

♓ ♈ ◑

17 Thursday

Last Quarter Moon ♈ ◑

18 Friday

Last Quarter Moon ♈ ♉ ◑

19 Saturday

♉ ◑

20 Sunday

♉ ♊ ◑

New Moon in Leo

KEY WORDS AND IDEAS FOR THIS LUNATION:

- Blow something up
- Be proud
- Don't be too proud!
- Say it again

DATE AND TIME OF THIS NEW MOON

LA: Jul 24, 12:11 | New York: Jul 24, 15:11 | London: Jul 24, 20:11 | Sydney: Jul 25, 05:11

The first thing to be aware of this New Moon is that it's a powerful one, because it's taking place exactly opposite Pluto, the planet of passion, paranoia, eruptions, and detoxification. If you're trying to create something new in your life and you need to blast away the old, now is the time.

We don't get chances like this all the time – this is a New Moon where you really can press the restart button on your health. As they say, 'If you don't make time for your wellness, you'll be forced to make time for your illness.'

This New Moon, don't just detox your body, but also detox your mind.

Work with the Dark Moon, which occurs on July 23 in the hours just before the New Moon, to get rid of any toxicity in your life. Set the intention to release it. Journal about it and burn the paper, or do breath work. I've included an exercise on the following page to help you with this. Over the years, I've started to work more and more with the Dark Moon and I know many of my readers adore doing the same. Take the time to breathe out anything that's upsetting you. The more you released and let go at the Full Moon earlier this month, and release again at the Dark Moon, the better.

And whatever happens, be proud of yourself this Leo New Moon. Not too proud, as that could set you up for pride before a fall, but, for example, if you do the breathing exercise on the following page once a day for a week, or you detox your diet, or even a friendship, be proud of yourself. Pat yourself on the back. I'd say reward yourself, but make sure your reward doesn't retox you!

Alternate Nostril Breathing Exercise

Breathwork is one of the most powerful ways to detox! My friend Michael James Wong gave me this super-simple breathwork exercise – a balancing, breathing practice in which each nostril is alternately used for inhalation and exhalation. This practice helps to calm the nervous system, balance masculine and feminine energy, balance left and right hemispheres of the brain, foster mental clarity, and aid concentration. Find a comfortable seat before starting.

1. Cover your right nostril with your right thumb and take a long slow inhale through your left nostril.
2. Use your right ring finger to close off your left nostril, and at the same time release your thumb from the right nostril.
3. Exhale through your right nostril, pause briefly at the end of the exhale, then inhale again through the right nostril.
4. Close off your right nostril with your right thumb, open your left and exhale through the left.
5. This completes one round. Repeat for several rounds of breath.

How to Work with This Moon

To discover where the energy of this New Moon is for you, find your Star sign or Rising sign here, see which House is involved, and then read The New Moon through the Houses (*see pages 12–15*): Aries – 5th House; Taurus – 4th House; Gemini – 3rd House; Cancer – 2nd House; Leo – 1st House; Virgo – 12th House; Libra – 11th House; Scorpio – 10th House; Sagittarius – 9th House; Capricorn – 8th House; Aquarius – 7th House; Pisces – 6th House.

NEW MOON WISHES AND INTENTIONS

My current biggest, most audacious goal, wish, or intention is:

Now turn it into an affirmation. Write it here as if it's already happened, and keep repeating it until the Full Moon.

Action steps I'm going to take toward this goal:

In the next 24 hours

In the coming week

In the month ahead

Tip: Write these actions as reminders on the diary pages.

I commit to this goal wholeheartedly!

Sign here:

This Week

The New Moon this week is blowing away all the old cobwebs – try to embrace change in a 'phoenix rising from the ashes' kind of way!

July 22: Sun into Leo

July 23: Dark Moon

July 24/25: New Moon occurs at 02°Leo08'

Quote of the Week

'If you keep good food in your fridge, you will eat good food.'

Errick McAdams,
American Council on Exercise certified personal trainer

July – Week 30

21 Monday

♊

22 Tuesday

♊ ♋

23 Wednesday

♋

24 Thursday

New Moon: LA: 12:11 | New York: 15:11 | London: 20:11 ♋ ♌

25 Friday

New Moon: Sydney: 05:11 ♌

26 Saturday

♌ ♍

27 Sunday

♍

This Week

This week could take a bit of a funny turn as it unfolds with some people being less nice than we might hope.

July 30: Chiron goes retrograde in Aries

July 31: Venus moves into Cancer

August 1: First Quarter Moon occurs at 09°Scorpio31′

What Are You Grateful For This Week?

July–August – Week 31

28 Monday

♍

---

29 Tuesday

♍ ♎

---

30 Wednesday

♎

---

31 Thursday

♎ ♏

---

1 Friday

First Quarter Moon ♏

---

2 Saturday

♏

---

3 Sunday

♏ ♐

August

August 1: First Quarter Moon in Scorpio

August 9: Full Moon in Aquarius

August 15/16: Last Quarter Moon in Taurus

August 22/23: Black New Moon in Virgo

August 30/31: First Quarter Moon in Sagittarius

How much change do you want in your life right now? Hopefully, the changes that came your way in the first half of the year have worked out really well for you, but if you've been left reeling, you have my full sympathy. There have been so many massive astrological shifts this year, and when the astrological landscape changes dramatically, sometimes our lives do too. So if you're still adjusting to change in your life and the last thing you want is more change, then take a deep breath....

This month brings two massive astrological alignments. In order to understand how important they are, I just want to give you a two-sentence astrology lesson. Basically, fast-moving planets such as Mercury, Venus, and Mars all speed around, aligning with each other on a regular basis. But the slower-moving outer planets – Jupiter, Saturn, Uranus, Neptune, and Pluto – rarely align with each other, and when they do it's huge news.

This month, outer planets Saturn and Uranus harmoniously align with each other, as do Neptune and Uranus. In a nutshell, this is all about hard work leading to positive change that is mystical and magical. It's the perfect time to renew the structures of our lives and wake up to our mystical powers.

Note that these two alignments aren't going to change the landscape. In fact, what they're going to do is help us get used to any changes that have taken place in our life and to see why, ultimately, they're all in our favor.

This month I will:

- ❑ **Break my routines**
- ❑ **Work on my spiritual side**
- ❑ **Wake up and smell the coffee**

Full Moon in Aquarius

KEY WORDS AND IDEAS FOR THIS LUNATION:

- Work smarter, not harder
- Chase your dreams
- Love to love
- Be detached

DATE AND TIME OF THIS FULL MOON

LA: Aug 9, 00:55 | New York: Aug 9, 03:55 | London: Aug 9, 08:55 | Sydney: Aug 9, 17:55

One thing to be aware of is that the Full Moon in Aquarius is always a good time to detach a little bit from your emotions. Full Moons tend to be highly emotional, but Aquarius is the most cool and aloof sign of the zodiac. Remember, this is never a criticism. We all have the sign of Aquarius in our chart somewhere.

It's almost as though you can lightly throw yourself into things at this Full Moon without worrying about being carried away by an emotional tidal wave.

Feel all your feelings, and process them in as pragmatic a way as possible, because Aquarius is nothing if not pragmatic.

It's also very much a time to chase your dreams, especially, but not only, dreams related to your working life. This is because the Full Moon is taking place as Mars, Saturn, and Neptune align. If you feel like you're being guided toward your right path by a Higher Power, then you might be right. Release what no longer serves you under the Full Moon and you'll tap into the Mars/Neptune energies more easily.

If you're on a spiritual path, then now is the time to be proactive. Be more motivated about meditation, take action toward connecting with your higher self, and be determined when it comes to creating a spiritual practice. If you tune in to the energies of this Full Moon, you're likely to get good results.

Also note this Full Moon takes place just before the current Mercury retrograde cycle ends on August 11. Clarity may be closer than you think.

Don't Be a Cling-On

If you're into manifesting, then you already know that doing what Gabrielle Bernstein calls 'manic manifesting' is one sure way to push your dreams away from you. Another way to describe this is the idea that if you chase a dog, they'll often run away from you. Whereas if you call the dog to you quietly while staying in the same spot, they'll often come to you. So under this Full Moon, do an honest inventory with yourself about where you've been clinging on to someone or something and become a bit manic in your manifesting. Make a conscious decision to detach and be less clingy. Your manifestation skills will thank you later!

How to Work with This Moon

To discover where the energy of this Full Moon is for you, find your Star sign or Rising sign here, see which House is involved, and then read The Full Moon through the Houses (see *pages 16–19*): Aries – 11th House; Taurus – 10th House; Gemini – 9th House; Cancer – 8th House; Leo – 7th House; Virgo – 6th House; Libra – 5th House; Scorpio – 4th House; Sagittarius – 3rd House; Capricorn – 2nd House; Aquarius – 1st House; Pisces – 12th House.

FULL MOON FORGIVENESS AND QUESTIONS TO ASK

This looks like it's going to be a very empowering Full Moon, and it's all the better for us to do our forgiveness and release work feeling on top of the world. So take a couple of deep breaths, and as you release them, decide that you're breathing out stress. And then answer the following questions.

Where have you been putting in your biggest efforts, and can you see that they're starting to pay off? Sometimes just acknowledging that makes anything you're manifesting even easier.

Do you have one dream in particular that you think is never going to happen? Does it feel like an impossible dream? If so, can you change your mindset around that or perhaps move on from it?

Romance in the air this Full Moon week. If you're open to love, how are you going to work with the energies?

This Week

There are five planetary aspects this week, and they all involve the planet of action, Mars. So whatever it is you're trying to achieve, you can take big strides forward.

August 6: Mars into Libra

August 9: Full Moon occurs at 17°Aquarius00′

Quote of the Week

'The measure of intelligence is the ability to change.'

Albert Einstein

August – Week 32

4 Monday

♐

5 Tuesday

♐♑

6 Wednesday

♑

7 Thursday

♑

8 Friday

♑♒

9 Saturday

Full Moon: LA: 00:55 | New York: 03:55 | London: 08:55 | Sydney: 17:55 ♒

10 Sunday

♒♓

This Week

Work hard for whatever you want this week, and something that's been stuck for a very long time could finally get unstuck and start to shift – in a really good way!

August 11: Mercury direct in Leo

August 12: Saturn harmonizes with Uranus

August 15/16: Last Quarter Moon occurs at 23°Taurus36'

What Are You Grateful For This Week?

August – Week 33

11 Monday

♓ ○

12 Tuesday

♓ ♈ ○

13 Wednesday

♈ ○

14 Thursday

♈ ♉ ◑

15 Friday

Last Quarter Moon ♉ ◑

16 Saturday

Last Quarter Moon ♉ ♊ ◑

17 Sunday

♊ ◑

New Moon in Virgo

KEY WORDS AND IDEAS FOR THIS LUNATION:

- Clashes
- Mind your manners
- Spiritual practice reboot
- Don't say too much

DATE AND TIME OF THIS NEW MOON

LA: Aug 22, 23:06 | New York: Aug 23, 02:06 | London: Aug 23, 07:06 | Sydney: Aug 23, 16:06

If you're into astrology, then you might be aware that Virgo is the most mild and managed sign of the zodiac. And before you go judging your Virgo friends, remember we all have Virgo in our chart somewhere. For you, Virgo is in whichever part of your chart that's listed in How to Work with This Moon on the following page.

But this isn't just any old Virgo New Moon. Normally, the Virgo New Moon is the perfect time to get organized and start again when it comes to being practical and getting s*** done. But this one is different because it's clashing almost perfectly with the planet of chaos and unexpected events, Uranus. This isn't strictly an astrological truth, but I think it's fair to say that Virgo and Uranus are absolute opposites.

The sign of Virgo is reliable and chaste and wants to do the right thing, whereas the planet Uranus couldn't care less about what anyone else thinks and does exactly what it wants.

Somewhat modifying this clash with Uranus is that almost straight afterward the Moon harmonizes with lucky Jupiter. So it could be a case of what shocks you one day makes you happier the next. Expect the unexpected, but also prepare to feel a sense of liberation

This New Moon is a great time to wake up and smell the coffee if you've been asleep as someone may be trying to pull a fast one. It's also a fantastic time to liberate yourself from a situation that feels cloying. Overall, be aware there could be some shocks and surprises around.

How Stressed Are You About Your Stress?

According to Stanford psychologist Kelly McGonigal in *The Upside of Stress*, it's our *reaction* to stress that has a greater impact on our health (and our future success) than the stress itself. There are a lot of quite stressful energies around this New Moon. There could easily be some curveballs and other events that you just didn't see coming. See if you can start to deal with the stress rather than your fears around the stress, though. If you find yourself saying 'I'm so stressed!' try to find a practical solution to your problem rather than talking about how stressed you are. Making a to-do list is the absolutely fundamental first step toward a stress solution.

How to Work with This Moon

To discover where the energy of this New Moon is for you, find your Star sign or Rising sign here, see which House is involved, and then read The New Moon through the Houses (*see pages 12–15*): Aries – 6th House; Taurus – 5th House; Gemini – 4th House; Cancer – 3rd House; Leo – 2nd House; Virgo – 1st House; Libra – 12th House; Scorpio – 11th House; Sagittarius – 10th House; Capricorn – 9th House; Aquarius – 8th House; Pisces – 7th House.

NEW MOON WISHES AND INTENTIONS

My current biggest, most audacious goal, wish, or intention is:

Now turn it into an affirmation. Write it here as if it's already happened, and keep repeating it until the Full Moon.

Action steps I'm going to take toward this goal:

In the next 24 hours

In the coming week

In the month ahead

Tip: Write these actions as reminders on the diary pages.

I commit to this goal wholeheartedly!

Sign here:

This Week

There's a New Moon taking place this week, but it could cause just a little bit of chaos! Note that it's called a Black Moon (because it's the third New Moon in a season with four New Moons).

August 22: Sun into Virgo; Dark Moon

August 22/23: Black New Moon occurs at 00°Virgo23′

Quote of the Week

'Stress can be a good thing –
if you choose to see it that way.'

Harvard Business Review

August – Week 34

18 Monday

♊ ♋

19 Tuesday

♋

20 Wednesday

♋ ♌

21 Thursday

♌

22 Friday

New Moon: LA: 23:06 ♌

23 Saturday

New Moon: New York: 02:06 | London: 07:06 | Sydney: 16:06 ♌ ♍

24 Sunday

♍

This Week

An absolutely fantastic week for using your imagination to create your future, changing up your spiritual practices, and enjoying a quick turn of events that leaves you feeling inspired.

August 25: Venus into Leo

August 29: Uranus harmonizes with Neptune

August 30/31: First Quarter Moon occurs at 08°Sagittarius07′

What Are You Grateful For This Week?

____

____

____

____

____

August – Week 35

25 Monday

♍ ♎

26 Tuesday

♎

27 Wednesday

♎

28 Thursday

♎ ♏

29 Friday

♏

30 Saturday

First Quarter Moon ♏ ♐

31 Sunday

First Quarter Moon ♐

September

September 7/8: Full Moon eclipse in Pisces

September 14: Last Quarter Moon in Gemini

September 21/22: New Moon eclipse in Virgo

September 29/30: First Quarter Moon in Capricorn

There are some months when not much is happening and we all get a chance to draw breath – but this isn't one of those months! There's so much going on in September, we can all expect to be feeling pretty darned busy or put-upon or drained, exhausted, exhilarated, or about a dozen other things in between!

The month kicks off with Saturn changing signs (again) and moving out of Aries and back into Pisces. If Saturn being in Pisces sounds familiar, that's because it took up residence there most recently from March 2023 to May 2025. It's now retrograding back to where it'll stay until February next year. So it's a last chance to do the hard work in your life (Saturn is all about hard work) that you need to do to grow as a person (Saturn is also all about growing up). To find out where Saturn is for you, check which House is involved for you during the New Moon in Pisces (see *page 64*). The same part of your life is being given this last chance to do the right thing, pay your dues, and pass some life tests.

But wait, there's more!

On top of this quite major news this month, we also get two eclipses: the first is a Full Moon eclipse on September 7, and the second is a New Moon eclipse on September 21. Remember, eclipses are when portals to another life open up – all the better for you to walk through them and see if you like your life more like that. And if you don't? Truthfully, it's not that easy to backtrack from an eclipse, so play carefully!

This month I will:

- ❑ **Do the work**
- ❑ **End something**
- ❑ **Start something**

Full Moon eclipse in Pisces

KEY WORDS AND IDEAS FOR THIS LUNATION:

- Slam a door shut
- Move on
- Let go
- Release

DATE AND TIME OF THIS FULL MOON ECLIPSE

LA: Sep 7, 11:08 | New York: Sep 7, 14:08 | London: Sep 7, 19:08 | Sydney: Sep 8, 04:08

Full Moon eclipses are about nothing if not slamming a door shut, moving on, letting go, and releasing. Here's the thing: If you resist doing this when your soul knows you need to, the eclipse becomes much harder to handle than if you graciously accept that was then and this is now. Eclipses are about getting us back on track with our lives when we've drifted from the path set for us before we incarnated here on the planet.

This Full Moon eclipse is in the sign of Pisces. Eagle-eyed readers will pick up on the fact that this is the same part of your chart where serious taskmaster Saturn has just reappeared. In other words, whichever part of your chart is being triggered by Saturn and this eclipse is where you have some serious personal growth to do. Happily, the eclipse is making a harmonious aspect to Jupiter, the planet of All Good Things.

Even though eclipses can be hard to handle, what happens at the time nearly always works out for the best.

One of the best things you can do for yourself during this lunation is to keep your thoughts positive. This doesn't mean spiritual bypassing; it means feel your feelings at the time of the Full Moon, process them, and then reach for the most positive thought you can. Focus on the many good things in your life. This should be reasonably easy thanks to a Mercury/Jupiter alignment happening just after the lunation.

Just to add a special note for UK readers – this eclipse will be visible from the UK.

Formula for Forgiveness

The following is a super-powerful incantation from my book *Moonology*™, which I'd urge you to say silently or out loud just before, during, or after the eclipse.

> *Under the glorious Full Moon, I forgive everything, everyone, every experience, and every memory of the past or present that needs forgiveness. I forgive positively everyone. I also forgive myself for past mistakes.*
>
> *The Universe is love, and I am forgiven and governed by love alone. Love is now adjusting my life. Realizing this, I abide in peace. I bring love and healing to all my thoughts, beliefs, and relationships. I learn my lessons and move on. I call on my soul fragments to be cleansed by the Full Moon, and I call on them to rejoin me. I send love to myself and everyone I know, and everyone who knows me in all directions of time.*
>
> *Under this glorious Full Moon, I am healed. My life is healed.*
>
> *And so it is. So be it.*

How to Work with This Moon

To discover where the energy of this Full Moon eclipse is for you, find your Star sign or Rising sign here, see which House is involved, and then read The Full Moon through the Houses (see *pages 16–19*): Aries – 12th House; Taurus – 11th House; Gemini – 10th House; Cancer – 9th House; Leo – 8th House; Virgo – 7th House; Libra – 6th House; Scorpio – 5th House; Sagittarius – 4th House; Capricorn – 3rd House; Aquarius – 2nd House; Pisces – 1st House.

FULL MOON FORGIVENESS AND QUESTIONS TO ASK

Every Full Moon is the right time to let go and move on. It's also the right time to forgive. But a Full Moon eclipse, which we have now, is that plus. So this month, practice some radical forgiveness and see if it comes easily to you.

Looking at the part of your life being triggered by the eclipse, what do you need to learn?

Is there someone or something you're hanging on to for grim death that you know you need to release? What is it, and are you willing to let it go?

Do you understand that if you let go of toxic things now at the Full Moon, you'll be in a much better position to start to make some powerful wishes at the New Moon eclipse in two weeks? How would your life look if you released that which is toxic?

This Week

The month kicks off with Saturn changing signs and the Full Moon eclipse. If you want to change your life, be intentional, release the past, and be disciplined about your spiritual practice.

September 1: Saturn retrogrades into Pisces

September 2: Mercury into Virgo

September 6: Uranus retrograde begins

September 7/8: Full Moon eclipse occurs at 15°Pisces23′

Quote of the Week

'That was then, this is now.'

S. E. Hinton, author

September – Week 36

1 Monday

♐ ◐

2 Tuesday

♐ ♑ ◐

3 Wednesday

♑ ◐

4 Thursday

♑ ♒ ○

5 Friday

♒ ○

6 Saturday

♒ ♓ ○

7 Sunday

Full Moon: LA: 11:08 | New York: 14:08 | London: 19:08

♓ ○

This Week

It's not always easy to look on the bright side of life, but this week the skies are supporting you to do just that, so have a go – you'll manifest better!

September 14: Last Quarter Moon occurs at 21°Gemini52′

What Are You Grateful For This Week?

September – Week 37

8 Monday

Full Moon: Sydney: 04:08 ♓♈○

9 Tuesday

♈○

10 Wednesday

♈♉○

11 Thursday

♉◯

12 Friday

♉♊◯

13 Saturday

♊◑

14 Sunday

Last Quarter Moon ♊◑

New Moon eclipse in Virgo

KEY WORDS AND IDEAS FOR THIS LUNATION:

- Tidy up
- Declutter
- Last chance
- Lessons learned

DATE AND TIME OF THIS NEW MOON ECLIPSE

LA: Sep 21, 12:54 | New York: Sep 21, 15:54 | London: Sep 21, 20:54 | Sydney: Sep 22, 05:54

On one hand, it's a little strange to suggest that if you want to make the most of this eclipse, you should take some time to tidy up your place. Eclipses are like magical portals to a new life, so would anyone really want to use up that amazing eclipse energy with a tidy-up? Perhaps not, but the Virgo energy of this New Moon is strong, so you might find that if you get your house in order around now, you'll also start to get your life in order, which can only be a good thing!

When your house or life is filled with clutter, it's very hard for positive energies to flow properly through your life.

Think of the difference between a stagnant pool and a wonderful fresh, rushing waterfall, and you get the idea of the 'before and after' if you use this New Moon to declutter.

Many feng shui experts say – and I tend to agree – that when our lives are cluttered, we can't manifest very well. So do make the most of this New Moon in the decluttering sign of Virgo to supercharge your manifesting powers.

Don't want to declutter? This is New Moon to think about the lessons that the last six months have taught you.

With all that said, remember that eclipses are amazing times. This is a chance to start over – take it seriously! Where in your life do you need a restart? Don't let this chance for change pass you by. On the next page, check where the eclipse is triggering your chart and really work on a restart in that part of your life.

Declutter Time!

If you've never tried it, go all Marie Kondo and look through all your stuff that you need to get rid of. Broadly speaking, the idea is to work out which items 'spark joy.' In other words, in looking through all your 'stuff,' what makes you feel something lovely and what is just junk that you're hanging on to for all the wrong reasons (e.g., you haven't had a moment to sort through everything, or you're keeping it 'just in case')? I can almost guarantee you that the more you declutter, the more your life will change. It's as though all our 'stuff' keeps us stuck in the past. Pass whatever you don't keep to someone else who might need it, or upcycle or recycle it if you can.

How to Work with This Moon

To discover where the energy of this New Moon eclipse is for you, find your Star sign or Rising sign here, see which House is involved, and then read The New Moon through the Houses (*see pages 12–15*): Aries – 6th House; Taurus – 5th House; Gemini – 4th House; Cancer – 3rd House; Leo – 2nd House; Virgo – 1st House; Libra – 12th House; Scorpio – 11th House; Sagittarius – 10th House; Capricorn – 9th House; Aquarius – 8th House; Pisces – 7th House.

NEW MOON WISHES AND INTENTIONS

My current biggest, most audacious goal, wish, or intention is:

____

____

Now turn it into an affirmation. Write it here as if it's already happened, and keep repeating it until the Full Moon.

____

____

Action steps I'm going to take toward this goal:

In the next 24 hours

____

In the coming week

____

In the month ahead

____

Tip: Write these actions as reminders on the diary pages.

I commit to this goal wholeheartedly!

Sign here:

____

This Week

It's a New Moon eclipse week, so it's an amazing time to set some super-powerful intentions – careful what you wish for, because you seriously might get it!

September 18: Mercury into Libra

September 19: Venus into Virgo

September 20: Dark Moon

September 21/22: New Moon eclipse occurs at 29°Virgo05′

Quote of the Week

'Keep only those things that speak to your heart.'

Marie Kondo,
The Life-Changing Magic of Tidying Up

September – Week 38

15 Monday

♊ ♋

16 Tuesday

♋

17 Wednesday

♋ ♌

18 Thursday

♌

19 Friday

♌ ♍

20 Saturday

♍

21 Sunday

New Moon: LA: 12:54 | New York: 15:54 | London: 20:54

♍ ♎

This Week

We're out of the eclipse season now, so life should be easier to handle – well, it *should* be, but will it be? A Mars/Pluto clash this week could be a bit of a fly in that ointment.

September 22: Mars into Scorpio; Sun into Libra;
Autumn Equinox in the northern hemisphere (Mabon);
Spring Equinox in the southern hemisphere (Ostara)

What Are You Grateful For This Week?

September – Week 39

22 Monday

New Moon: Sydney: 05:54

♎

23 Tuesday

♎

24 Wednesday

♎ ♏↗

25 Thursday

♏↗

26 Friday

♏↗ ♐

27 Saturday

♐

28 Sunday

♐

October

October 6/7: Full Moon in Aries

October 13/14: Last Quarter Moon in Cancer

October 21: New Moon in Libra

October 29/30: First Quarter Moon in Aquarius

And just like that, the astrological landscape changes again as Neptune retrogrades back into Pisces for the rest of the year. It's been a year of change, and it's not over yet! So what does this mean for us all?

Neptune is the planet of confusion and deception. It's also one of the hardest planets to write about because it's the planet of mists and air. Trying to understand Neptune is like trying to grab oxygen with your hand. It's the planet of dreams, soulmates, and enlightenment, but also of lies, disappointment, and illicit affairs.

Let's focus on the positive here, though!

Neptune has been in the dreamy sign of Pisces since 2011. This is perhaps the main reason, planetarily speaking, why meditation, chanting, intuitive work, yoga, breath work, and other such pursuits have come to the fore. It was something of a double whammy. The most mystical planet has been in the most mystical sign of the zodiac.

In March this year, you may recall that Neptune shifted into Aries and now is retrograding back into Pisces for a last hurrah. One of the best ways to tune in to this energy is to up your spiritual practice – aim for it to be working so well that you can take it with you seamlessly into the Neptune in Aries cycle, which starts in January 2026 and lasts until 2039.

So this month, ask yourself what spirituality means to you. Do you believe you're creating your own reality? Do you feel you're down here in 3D reality and connected to a higher power? Tune in.

This month I will:

- ❑ **Meditate, meditate, meditate**
- ❑ **Commune with the Divine**
- ❑ **Work through confusion**

This Week

If one of your most important relationships is troubled right now, use this week to shower each other with love and talk through your issues. This applies to romantic and platonic relationships.

September 29: St. Michael's Feast (Michaelmas)

September 29/30: First Quarter Moon occurs at 7°Capricorn05′

What Are You Grateful For This Week?

September – October – Week 40

29 Monday

First Quarter Moon ♐ ♑ ◐

30 Tuesday

First Quarter Moon ♑ ◐

1 Wednesday

♑ ♒ ◐

2 Thursday

♒ ◐

3 Friday

♒ ○

4 Saturday

♒ ♓ ○

5 Sunday

♓ ○

Full Moon in Aries

KEY WORDS AND IDEAS FOR THIS LUNATION:

- End one cycle
- Work through arguments
- Detox mentally
- Love to love

DATE AND TIME OF THIS FULL MOON

LA: Oct 6, 20:47 | New York: Oct 6, 23:47 | London: Oct 7, 04:47 | Sydney: Oct 7, 14:47

Sometimes we get so wound up in arguments with the people in our lives (especially with the people we love) that we lose sight of how much we care. Then we start to take them for granted, and before we know it, the whole thing has exploded. Watch out this month if you're in that situation. The Full Moon is taking place in the fiery sign of Aries, which is already a lot! Aries is the first sign of the zodiac and has a childlike quality. And what do kids do? They think they're the center of the Universe and act accordingly! So mind how you behave if you've been doing a little bit of that lately.

At the time of this Full Moon, communications planet Mercury and furious and destructive Pluto are at odds with each other.

Normally, this might be expressed as a passing moment of upset, but because it takes place just after the Full Moon it's time to think twice before you get into conflict with someone. Think about how well or not you're communicating, and do something about it if you need to. Don't push your emotions down around the Full Moon; feel them and work through them.

The Full Moon always takes place when the Sun and Moon are on opposite sides of the zodiac. In the case of Aries, the opposite sign is the partnership sign of Libra, so go easy in all your most important relationships – romantic, professional, or otherwise.

The good news is that after the Full Moon and the Mercury/ Pluto clash, we get a lovely alignment between Venus and Jupiter. Venus is the love planet, and Jupiter is the 'lots of' planet, so put them together and you can move toward a much more loving space.

Accept Yourself

Under this Full Moon, it's more important than ever to accept yourself for who you are – which is hopefully someone who is trying to do the right thing in life and better themselves. This month, under the Full Moon, honor the darkness being lit up by the lunation. Find yourself a candle – black, if possible – and under the Full Moon (just before, during, or after), light it up and sit in front of it with your body 'open' to it. In other words, perhaps sit in the lotus position in front of it, but at the very least, don't cross your arms or legs. And just breathe. Breathe in love for yourself, and breathe out any negativity. Do it for at least five minutes.

How to Work with This Moon

To discover where the energy of this Full Moon is for you, find your Star sign or Rising sign here, see which House is involved, and then read The Full Moon through the Houses (*see pages 16–19*): Aries – 1st House; Taurus – 12th House; Gemini – 11th House; Cancer – 10th House; Leo – 9th House; Virgo – 8th House; Libra – 7th House; Scorpio – 6th House; Sagittarius – 5th House; Capricorn – 4th House; Aquarius – 3rd House; Pisces – 2nd House.

FULL MOON FORGIVENESS AND QUESTIONS TO ASK

Most of us are lucky enough to be able to say that no one gives us as hard a time as we give ourselves. Maybe this isn't quite true for you – perhaps you've really been through the mill. Even so, are you always kind to yourself? Work on this now.

What have I done that's impacted me or others, and can I forgive myself for it?

Who has hurt me most this year or ever, and can I forgive them for it?

What would my life look like if I could forgive myself and others?

This Week

This Full Moon week brings with it a chance to clear your mind out. 'Thinking happier thoughts' sounds a little facile, but it'll change your life and make you a more powerful manifester.

October 6: Mercury into Scorpio

October 6/7: Full Moon occurs at 14°Aries08'

Quote of the Week

'Say what you mean, but don't say it mean.'

ANDREA WACHTER, MARRIAGE COUNSELOR

October – Week 41

6 Monday

Full Moon: LA: 20:47 | New York: 23:47 ♓♈○

7 Tuesday

Full Moon: London: 04:47 | Sydney: 14:47 ♈○

8 Wednesday

♈♉○

9 Thursday

♉○

10 Friday

♉♊○

11 Saturday

♊○

12 Sunday

♊♋◑

This Week

There's a lot of room for romance this week – as long as you're with someone you can trust. Love with your whole heart (but don't be a fool for love!).

October 13: Venus moves into Libra

October 13/14: Last Quarter Moon occurs at 20°Cancer39'

October 14: Pluto retrograde ends

What Are You Grateful For This Week?

October – Week 42

13 Monday

Last Quarter Moon ♋

14 Tuesday

Last Quarter Moon ♋♌

15 Wednesday

♌

16 Thursday

♌♍

17 Friday

♍

18 Saturday

♍

19 Sunday

♍♎

New Moon in Libra

KEY WORDS AND IDEAS FOR THIS LUNATION:

- Relationship restart
- Out with the old
- Relationship detox
- Mysticism revisited

DATE AND TIME OF THIS NEW MOON

LA: Oct 21, 05:25 | New York: Oct 21, 08:25 | London: Oct 21, 13:25 | Sydney: Oct 21, 23:25

The New Moon in Libra happens once a year, and on the surface it brings a chance to start all over again in at least one important relationship. As you read this, which relationship do you feel might need a restart? Could it also need a detox? Unfortunately, this New Moon is also making what's called an 'out-of-sign' clash with Pluto which, as we've talked about, is the detox planet. It's also the planet of muck and mess; think of it as the plumber of the zodiac, unblocking a nasty, messed-up pipeline.

Think about where in your life a relationship has gone toxic and needs clearing, but don't wade in without some kind of intention or it might get messy!

It's a very good New Moon to set intentions about your love life, but have you cleared away the debris from the past yet? It's also a great time to make a wish about how you want your relationships to be in the future. Just be sure you're not allowing bad experiences from the past to muddy your present and therefore your future.

There's a lot of healing around now, but it's more likely to be expressed as a healing crisis – in other words, an upset that ultimately leads to better things, the same way a blocked sink (continuing the plumbing analogy!) can ultimately lead to clear pipes. Sorry it's all a little yucky, but that's the flavor of this lunation.

The New Moon also takes place the day before Neptune retrogrades back into Pisces. Neptune and Pisces both have a rather cloudy and surreal feel to them so confusion may arise in some areas of your life, but it can also be an amazing time to connect spiritually.

Cleansing Light

Set aside 15–20 minutes. Search online or on whichever platform you listen to music on for 582 Hz music, which is said to help reduce anxiety. Close your eyes and just breathe. And breathe. Listen to the music and let it wash over you. Once you feel your nervous system start to calm down, it's time to bring in a visualization. Envisage a column of bright white light tinged with the palest of blues and specks of gold, pouring down from the heavens to you here on Earth. And breathe. Sit in this column of light and let it cleanse away whatever needs to be released. Visit my site (see *page 22*) for the full meditation.

How to Work with This Moon

To discover where the energy of this New Moon is for you, find your Star sign or Rising sign here, see which House is involved, and then read The New Moon through the Houses (see *pages 12–15*): Aries – 7th House; Taurus – 6th House; Gemini – 5th House; Cancer – 4th House; Leo – 3rd House; Virgo – 2nd House; Libra – 1st House; Scorpio – 12th House; Sagittarius – 11th House; Capricorn – 10th House; Aquarius – 9th House; Pisces – 8th House.

NEW MOON WISHES AND INTENTIONS

My current biggest, most audacious goal, wish, or intention is:

Now turn it into an affirmation. Write it here as if it's already happened, and keep repeating it until the Full Moon.

Action steps I'm going to take toward this goal:

In the next 24 hours

In the coming week

In the month ahead

Tip: Write these actions as reminders on the diary pages.

I commit to this goal wholeheartedly!

Sign here:

This Week

Neptune retrogrades back into Pisces this New Moon week. Use this opportunity to set intentions for your spiritual life and healing.

October 20: Dark Moon

October 21: New Moon occurs at 28°Libra22′

October 22: Neptune retrogrades into Pisces

October 23: Sun into Scorpio; Jupiter clashes with Chiron

October 24: St. Raphael's Feast

Quote of the Week

'What hurts us is what heals us.'

Paulo Coelho

October – Week 43

20 Monday

21 Tuesday

New Moon: LA: 05:25 | New York: 08:25 | London: 13:25 | Sydney: 23:25

22 Wednesday

23 Thursday

24 Friday

25 Saturday

26 Sunday

This Week

Tap into the extra cosmic vibrations this week with meditation, chanting, breath work, or whatever else works for you. Raise your vibration and watch your life evolve.

October 29: Mercury into Sagittarius

October 29/30: Quarter Moon occurs at 06°Aquarius30′

October 30/November 1: Samhain in the northern hemisphere; Beltane in the southern hemisphere

What Are You Grateful For This Week?

October – November – Week 44

27 Monday

28 Tuesday

29 Wednesday

First Quarter Moon

30 Thursday

First Quarter Moon

31 Friday

1 Saturday

2 Sunday

November

November 5/6: Full Moon in Taurus

November 11/12: Last Quarter Moon in Leo

November 19/20: New Moon in Scorpio

November 27/28: First Quarter Moon in Pisces

It's another big month with Mercury and Jupiter going retrograde, and Saturn and then Mercury going direct (which means ending their retrograde). Plus, we have Uranus already in retrograde, moving back into Taurus for a final fling and then connecting with Neptune, which is also retrograde. So where does all this leave us as we move into the penultimate month of the year?

For one thing, the retrograde energy means it's time for us to stop trying to race forward in life. Instead, use this month to take a breath. Yes, it's almost the end of the year, and yes, we're all excited for 2026, but allow a little light and shade. Think of this month as a chance to regroup before we hit December and get catapulted into the New Year.

Spend some time thinking back over the time since January and look at where you feel you've done well and where you wish you'd done things differently. Think about what lessons you've been taught – did you learn them, or did you just press forward without taking on board the advice the Universe was trying to transmit?

Mercury retrograde is a time to rethink, review, and revise. Jupiter retrograde is a time to re-enjoy, to go back to somewhere you've traveled before, for another chance to get lucky. Uranus retrograde means there's less ongoing chaos, but some old chaotic scenes could be revisited. Saturn going direct means a new slew of lessons is coming your way.

With so many energies, the only thing to do is to... live consciously.

This month I will:

- ❑ **Rethink, review, and revise**
- ❑ **Live and let live**
- ❑ **Assimilate my life lessons**

Super Full Moon in Taurus

KEY WORDS AND IDEAS FOR THIS LUNATION:

- Positive changes
- Create your own reality
- Financial bonus
- Feistiness

DATE AND TIME OF THIS SUPER FULL MOON

LA: Nov 5, 05:19 | New York: Nov 5, 08:19 | London: Nov 5, 13:19 | Sydney: Nov 6, 00:19

Now is the time to turn your mind to the age-old idea that's reemerged in the past few years: that we create our own reality. Do you understand this? Have you heard about it? Are you perhaps even very well versed in it?

As we move through this Full Moon, think about where in your life you've wanted something that came to pass. And where you've perhaps not been grateful for someone or something that's then slipped through your fingers. Think about where you made a dream real and where your fear manifested. These are all examples of how you created your own reality – we work with it subconsciously; however it's also possible to work with it consciously. And when we work with it consciously, that's when we become powerful creators of our own reality.

This Full Moon, do a deep dive into your feelings. Feelings are everything when it comes to creating your dream life.

Look at where you're hung up on the past, on someone or something you need to move on from, on a past resentment or jealousy or fear. Every emotion that's trapped in your body like this keeps you from emerging as the powerful being that you are. That's because trapped emotions take up so much space inside your energy field and push out the healthier, free-flowing emotions that would create your dream life.

So forgive and move on. Release paranoia and drama. The Full Moon in Taurus is the moment to see if you're stuck or taking a fixed position or refusing to release a grudge. Move through all that s***.

I'm Worth It!

This Full Moon is also a great time to turn the corner financially. Taurus is the sign associated with creature comforts. It's ruled by Venus, the planet of abundance, too. One of the best ways to create a better financial reality for yourself is to realize that you deserve it. It's become almost a cliché to say this now, but it's real and powerful. So this month under the Full Moon, grab a sheet of paper and write down as many things as you can think of about why you're a good person, why you're amazing, why you make the world a better place. Read this list over through the coming four weeks so you start to see – you really are worth it!

How to Work with This Moon

To discover where the energy of this Super Full Moon is for you, find your Star sign or Rising sign here, see which House is involved, and then read The Full Moon through the Houses (*see pages 16–19*): Aries – 2nd House; Taurus – 1st House; Gemini – 12th House; Cancer – 11th House; Leo – 10th House; Virgo – 9th House; Libra – 8th House; Scorpio – 7th House; Sagittarius – 6th House; Capricorn – 5th House; Aquarius – 4th House; Pisces – 3rd House.

FULL MOON FORGIVENESS AND QUESTIONS TO ASK

The Full Moon in Taurus happens when the Sun is in Taurus's opposite sign of Scorpio – and Scorpio is the sign that could hold a grudge for millennia. Remember, we all have Scorpio in our chart somewhere. You can find out where Scorpio is for you by casting your chart (see *page 22*) if you haven't already. Can you break free of this?

Who (if anyone) do you have a grudge against? Why? Can you let it go?

____

____

____

Can you see that holding a grudge keeps you stuck in the past? Does that make it easier to release?

____

____

How would you rate your current stress levels? We're nearing the end of the year when life often speeds up. Can you stop and take a breath now before the mayhem starts?

____

____

____

This Week

Mercury goes retrograde, and Uranus is already retrograde now, so make sure you back up anything you need to on your phone or computer, and prepare to start reviewing the year that was.

November 4: Mars into Sagittarius

November 5/6: Full Moon occurs at 13°Taurus23'

November 6: Venus into Scorpio

November 8: Uranus retrogrades back into Taurus

November 9: Mercury goes retrograde in Sagittarius

Quote of the Week

'Self-doubt is the biggest manifestation killer.'

Sonia Choquette

November – Week 45

3 Monday

♈○

4 Tuesday

♈♉○

5 Wednesday

Full Moon: LA: 05:19 | New York: 08:19 | London: 13:19 ♉○

6 Thursday

Full Moon: Sydney: 00:19 ♉♊○

7 Friday

♊○

8 Saturday

♊♋○

9 Sunday

♋○

This Week

Mercury retrograde meets Mars this week so be careful – an old argument might be about to come up again. Laughter is the best medicine in this scenario as Mercury and Mars are in comedy sign Sagittarius.

November 11: Jupiter goes retrograde in Cancer

November 11/12: Last Quarter Moon occurs at 20°Leo04′

What Are You Grateful For This Week?

November – Week 46

10 Monday

♋♌

11 Tuesday

Last Quarter Moon ♌

12 Wednesday

Last Quarter Moon ♌♍

13 Thursday

♍

14 Friday

♍

15 Saturday

♍♎

16 Sunday

♎

New Moon in Scorpio

KEY WORDS AND IDEAS FOR THIS LUNATION:

- Fast changes
- Rip off the Band-Aid
- Radical turnaround
- Second chances

DATE AND TIME OF THIS NEW MOON

LA: Nov 19, 22:47 | New York: Nov 20, 01:47 | London: Nov 20, 06:47 | Sydney: Nov 20, 17:47

This New Moon is a good one – it promises fast changes and radical turnarounds. If you've been feeling stuck and wishing more than anything that things would change, then be careful what you wish for, because things really could be about to change for you!

This New Moon in Scorpio is taking place exactly opposite the planet of change and liberation, of waking up and electricity, aka Uranus. It's a massive callout from the Universe to remind you that you're only as stuck as you think you are.

If you're in a difficult situation and you're trying to work out how to let go, this New Moon could be the time to do it.

Normally, we equate the Full Moon with the time to move on but this New Moon is so powerful, it's like ripping off a Band-Aid and starting again all in one fell swoop. Can you do it? If this is resonating with you, chances are that something needs to change.

There's also a sense that second chances are in the air now, as the New Moon is taking place right next to Mercury, which is retrograde. There could be surprising news – hopefully great news! It's also a good time to change your thoughts, and remember: if you change your thoughts, you can change your life.

This lunation also takes place on the same day as a very rare alignment: electric Uranus is connecting with mystical Neptune for the first time since 1993. Make a New Moon wish to become more enlightened and you just might get it! Tune in to any intuitive insights coming your way. It's also a good time to break free from any addictions you know are hampering you.

Belief-Breaking exercise

It's never good to get stuck in negative thoughts, and now is a great time to move through any negativity. One of the first ways to do this is the break your negative beliefs. Start by isolating a negative belief you have about yourself, such as 'I'm too fat/thin/young/old/I'm not good enough, etc....' And now counter it with something positive, such as 'That's BS! The truth is I can lose weight/gain weight/youth is a strength/age brings wisdom/I'm more than good enough,' and so on. This is one of my favorite exercises, and the swearing is vital because it shocks your brain a little bit (and sweary people live longer, so they say).

How to Work with This Moon

To discover where the energy of this New Moon is for you, find your Star sign or Rising sign here, see which House is involved, and then read The New Moon through the Houses (see *pages 12–15*): Aries – 8th House; Taurus – 7th House; Gemini – 6th House; Cancer – 5th House; Leo – 4th House; Virgo – 3rd House; Libra – 2nd House; Scorpio – 1st House; Sagittarius – 12th House; Capricorn – 11th House; Aquarius – 10th House; Pisces – 9th House.

NEW MOON WISHES AND INTENTIONS

My current biggest, most audacious goal, wish, or intention is:

Now turn it into an affirmation. Write it here as if it's already happened, and keep repeating it until the Full Moon.

Action steps I'm going to take toward this goal:

In the next 24 hours

In the coming week

In the month ahead

Tip: Write these actions as reminders on the diary pages.

I commit to this goal wholeheartedly!

Sign here:

This Week

This New Moon week offers a chance to get creative in visualizing the life you want and actually make it happen – you just have to believe it's possible!

November 19: Mercury into Scorpio; Dark Moon

November 19/20: New Moon occurs at 28°Scorpio12'; Uranus harmonizes with Neptune

November 22: Sun into Sagittarius

Quote of the Week

'You create your opportunities by asking for them.'

Shakti Gawain, *Creative Visualization*

November – Week 47

17 Monday

18 Tuesday

19 Wednesday

New Moon: LA: 22:47

20 Thursday

New Moon: New York: 01:47 | London: 06:47 | Sydney: 17:47

21 Friday

22 Saturday

23 Sunday

This Week

It's a week when saying something kind, sweet, or loving that you should have said earlier could really work for you – speak from your heart and good things can follow.

November 27/28: First Quarter Moon occurs at 06°Pisces17'

November 28: Saturn retrograde ends

November 29: Mercury retrograde ends

November 30: Venus into Sagittarius

What Are You Grateful For This Week?

November – Week 48

24 Monday

♑ ◐

---

25 Tuesday

♑ ♒ ◐

---

26 Wednesday

♒ ◐

---

27 Thursday

First Quarter Moon ♒ ♓ ◐

---

28 Friday

First Quarter Moon ♓ ◐

---

29 Saturday

♓ ◐

---

30 Sunday

♓ ♈ ◐

December

December 4/5: Full Moon in Gemini

December 11/12: Last Quarter Moon in Virgo

December 19/20: New Moon in Sagittarius

December 27/28: First Quarter Moon in Aries

It's not necessarily going to be the easiest end to the year. We've experienced 12 months of big astrological changes. Hopefully, most of them feel like they've worked in your favor, but if not, all you can do is try to take 2025 in your stride and know that life is changing and working *for* you, not against you.

Sometimes life sends us tests to see how much we want someone or something, and sometimes to see whether or not we've learned our lessons.

If you're going through a tough time now as the year ends, then at least be happy that you can soon put all this behind you. One of the worst things in life is regret. So try to work through any that you have. Forgive yourself if you wish you'd done something differently. Believe that the Universe is on your side. Try to surrender to Divine will if life is challenging you.

One message this month could be about how much you've put up with this year. Have you had enough? There's an intense alignment this month between amplifying Jupiter and the planetoid of healing, Chiron. It's a reminder that people can only do to us what we let them. If you've been hurt, draw a line and decide not to allow any more pain. Also decide to heal.

Please try not to feel deflated that 2025 isn't ending on a high. Sometimes we just need a moment like this to reflect on everything. If you can focus on the ways in which you're lucky, you've learned what you need to this year.

This month I will:

- ❑ **Draw a line**
- ❑ **Set boundaries**
- ❑ **Decide to heal**

Super Full Moon in Gemini

KEY WORDS AND IDEAS FOR THIS LUNATION:

- See the bigger picture
- Have a good flirt
- End an argument
- Start healing

DATE AND TIME OF THIS SUPER FULL MOON

LA: Dec 4, 15:14 | New York: Dec 4, 18:14 | London: Dec 4, 23:14 | Sydney: Dec 5, 10:14

It's the last Super Full Moon of the year – so what are you going to do with it? It's in the sign of Gemini, which is perfect because it allows us to release and let go of any negative thoughts that might otherwise come with us into 2026. And that's the last thing we want – to take anything difficult from this year into the next.

Yes, of course, years are 'man-made,' so to speak. They're just our way of understanding the passage of time. However, as much as they're not 'real' or organic, they're in the collective consciousness and do mean something.

It's not the new year yet, and you may or may not be someone who likes to make New Year's resolutions, but use this Full Moon in Gemini to clear your head of anything you know you need to release for your own wellbeing and mental health. Maybe it's a fear, a regret, shame over something, an upset, or something else. Just try as much as you can to face up to what is and know that you can create your own reality once you rid yourself of toxic thoughts.

Communication is strongly highlighted at this Full Moon, so if you need to talk things through with someone in the weeks ahead, don't hesitate.

Note that this Full Moon is also one of those times when there's a lot of healing in the air. If you're suffering mentally or physically, it's a good time to seek professional help, be it from a mainstream or alternative health practitioner. Talking therapy could be particularly useful right now. This is also a great time to work on adopting a more positive mindset.

Goodbye-to-All-That List

Every year I try to remember to encourage you to make a farewell list for the year. So here's your reminder. The idea is that intention is, of course, everything. So set the intention to leave behind anything from 2025 you don't want to take into your future. On the night of the Full Moon ideally, or as close to it as you can get, write a list of whatever it is that upset you this year and that you're leaving behind – then burn the list. This might seem like a morose exercise, but it'll work for you. Finally, to replace what you're releasing, write a list of the top 10 things you're grateful for.

How to Work with This Moon

To discover where the energy of this Super Full Moon is for you, find your Star sign or Rising sign here, see which House is involved, and then read The Full Moon through the Houses (see *pages 16–19*): Aries – 3rd House; Taurus – 2nd House; Gemini – 1st House; Cancer – 12th House; Leo – 11th House; Virgo – 10th House; Libra – 9th House; Scorpio – 8th House; Sagittarius – 7th House; Capricorn – 6th House; Aquarius – 5th House; Pisces – 4th House.

FULL MOON FORGIVENESS AND QUESTIONS TO ASK

If our thoughts lead to our actions and our actions lead to our karma, then it pays us to rid ourselves of negative thinking. Agreed? The irony is that sometimes we have to think about what we don't want to think about anymore to release it!

Who from 2025 do I need to forgive, and am I willing to?

They say that 'life doesn't happen to us; it happens for us.' Express how you feel about this idea in terms of the events of 2025.

Self-talk is also so important – as in, what are you telling yourself? Are you willing to release negative self-talk as the year ends? What kind things can you say to yourself instead?

This Week

This Full Moon week has lots of good things about it. For a start, if you've had ups and downs this year, a Mars/Chiron link is your cue to start the healing process.

December 4/5: Full Moon occurs at 13°Gemini04'

Quote of the Week

'Breathe, darling. This is just a chapter.
It's not your whole story.'

S. C. Lourie

December – Week 49

1 Monday

♈

2 Tuesday

♈♉

3 Wednesday

♉

4 Thursday

Full Moon: LA: 15:14 | New York: 18:14 | London: 23:14 ♉♊

5 Friday

Full Moon: Sydney: 10:14 ♊

6 Saturday

♊♋

7 Sunday

♋

This Week

Mind how you go this Quarter Moon week – there could be people in bad moods lecturing people who are feeling vulnerable. Try to avoid being on either side of that astrological equation.

December 10: Neptune retrograde ends in Pisces

December 11: Mercury into Sagittarius

December 11/12: Last Quarter Moon occurs at 20°Virgo04′

What Are You Grateful For This Week?

December – Week 50

8 Monday

♋♌

---

9 Tuesday

♌

---

10 Wednesday

♌♍

---

11 Thursday

Last Quarter Moon ♍

---

12 Friday

Last Quarter Moon ♍♎

---

13 Saturday

♎

---

14 Sunday

♎

New Moon in Sagittarius

KEY WORDS AND IDEAS FOR THIS LUNATION:

- Look on the bright side
- Don't overindulge!
- Love openly
- Be true

DATE AND TIME OF THIS NEW MOON

LA: Dec 19, 17:43 | New York: Dec 19, 20:43 | London: Dec 20, 01:43 | Sydney: Dec 20, 12:43

While there's no doubt that this New Moon has a challenging side, it also has a cheerful and positive flavor – focus on that if you can!

We're now in the part of the year unofficially known as 'the silly season.' At this time of the year, we tend to throw everything up in the air, almost as if to say, 'Well, that was the year that was – I can't do much about it now... Let's get a bit reckless!'

Just mind how you go, not least because this New Moon is clashing with Neptune – hard! There's a lot of room for deception, disappointment, drowning any sorrows, or just generally feeling misty-eyed and confused.

If there's a solution to all of this it's about being kind and compassionate as the year ends, even if you do slightly feel as though life is giving you lemons!

Love with an open heart, forgive others if they can't love you back in the same way, and be generous, even if people are being mean.

More than anything, be true to yourself, and you'll have the best possible chance of thriving. When you set your intentions this New Moon, make sure there are some big ones for the whole year ahead!

Note that this lunation is making what's known as an out-of-sign conjunction to the planet of feistiness and determination, Mars, so expect intense energy as people celebrate the end of the year. If you find yourself in a situation where someone has tipped over into straight-out anger, try using humor to defuse the situation.

Calling in Your Future

Do this exercise every morning for 14 days and see how you feel. Find a quiet space and sit comfortably. Start by taking three deep breaths to center yourself. Close your eyes and vividly imagine your desired future. See every detail; feel every emotion. As you visualize, tune in to the emotions and energy of that future self. Feel the joy, love, or abundance you desire. Speak out loud or silently affirm, 'I am now aligned with my future self and all its blessings.' Carry this aligned energy with you throughout the day, trusting that your future is on its way to you.

How to Work with This Moon

To discover where the energy of this New Moon is for you, find your Star sign or Rising sign here, see which House is involved, and then read The New Moon through the Houses (see *pages 12–15*): Aries – 9th House; Taurus – 8th House; Gemini – 7th House; Cancer – 6th House; Leo – 5th House; Virgo – 4th House; Libra – 3rd House; Scorpio – 12th House; Sagittarius – 1st House; Capricorn – 12th House; Aquarius – 11th House; Pisces – 10th House.

NEW MOON WISHES AND INTENTIONS

My current biggest, most audacious goal, wish, or intention is:

____

____

Now turn it into an affirmation. Write it here as if it's already happened, and keep repeating it until the Full Moon.

____

____

Action steps I'm going to take toward this goal:

In the next 24 hours

____

In the coming week

____

In the month ahead

____

Tip: Write these actions as reminders on the diary pages.

I commit to this goal wholeheartedly!

Sign here:

____

This Week

A tough Venus/Saturn link this New Moon week reminds us to honor ourselves and give anyone who doesn't do the same as wide a berth as we can!

December 15: Mars into Capricorn

December 19: Dark Moon

December 19/20: New Moon occurs at 28°Sagittarius25′

December 21: Jupiter clashes with Chiron; Sun into Capricorn; Summer Solstice in the southern hemisphere (Litha); Winter Solstice in the northern hemisphere (Yule)

Quote of the Week

'We don't laugh because we're happy; we're happy because we laugh.'

William James, philosopher, historian, and psychologist

December – Week 51

15 Monday

♎ ♏

---

16 Tuesday

♏

---

17 Wednesday

♏ ♐

---

18 Thursday

♐

---

19 Friday

New Moon: LA: 17:43 | New York: 20:43 ♐

---

20 Saturday

New Moon: London: 01:43 | Sydney: 12:43 ♐ ♑

---

21 Sunday

♑

This Week

Even if there are upsets this week, there's also good news: the planet of love, Venus, and the healing planetoid, Chiron, are aligning, so you can heal whatever is hurting.

December 24: Venus into Capricorn

December 27/28: First Quarter Moon occurs at 06°Aries17′

What Are You Grateful For This Week?

December – Week 52

22 Monday

♑ ♒

23 Tuesday

♒

24 Wednesday

♒

25 Thursday

♒ ♓

26 Friday

♓

27 Saturday

First Quarter Moon ♓ ♈

28 Sunday

First Quarter Moon ♈

This Week

There's a fiery Full Moon in the sign of Cancer this week. It's a great time to wrap up work projects and focus on your home and family. Just watch your temper if you tend toward the choleric!

January 1: Mercury into Capricorn

January 2: Chiron direct

January 3: Full Moon occurs at 13°Cancer01′

Mantra of the Week

Om Gam Ganapataye (pronounced Gan-a-pat-eye-ay) *Namaha*

This chant to the Hindu elephant God Ganesha is a much-loved mantra used all over India. I learned it at the Sri Narayani Peedam spiritual center in India, which I've been visiting since 2005. Even if you only chant it once, it brings positive energy to the start of anything new, including a new year!

December – January 2026 – Week 1

29 Monday

♈♉◐

30 Tuesday

♉◐

31 Wednesday

♉♊◐

1 Thursday

♊◐

2 Friday

♊♋◯

3 Saturday

Full Moon: LA: 02:03 | New York: 05:03 | London: 10:03 | Sydney: 21:03 ♋◯

4 Sunday

♋♌◯

JANUARY

M	T	W	T	F	S	S
			1	2	3	4
5	6	7	8	9	10	11
12	13	14	15	16	17	18
19	20	21	22	23	24	25
26	27	28	29	30	31	

FEBRUARY

M	T	W	T	F	S	S
						1
2	3	4	5	6	7	8
9	10	11	12	13	14	15
16	17	18	19	20	21	22
23	24	25	26	27	28	

MARCH

M	T	W	T	F	S	S
						1
2	3	4	5	6	7	8
9	10	11	12	13	14	15
16	17	18	19	20	21	22
23	24	25	26	27	28	29
30	31					

APRIL

M	T	W	T	F	S	S
		1	2	3	4	5
6	7	8	9	10	11	12
13	14	15	16	17	18	19
20	21	22	23	24	25	26
27	28	29	30			

MAY

M	T	W	T	F	S	S
				1	2	3
4	5	6	7	8	9	10
11	12	13	14	15	16	17
18	19	20	21	22	23	24
25	26	27	28	29	30	31

JUNE

M	T	W	T	F	S	S
1	2	3	4	5	6	7
8	9	10	11	12	13	14
15	16	17	18	19	20	21
22	23	24	25	26	27	28
29	30					

JULY						
M	T	W	T	F	S	S
		1	2	3	4	5
6	7	8	9	10	11	12
13	14	15	16	17	18	19
20	21	22	23	24	25	26
27	28	29	30	31		

AUGUST						
M	T	W	T	F	S	S
					1	2
3	4	5	6	7	8	9
10	11	12	13	14	15	16
17	18	19	20	21	22	23
24	25	26	27	28	29	30
31						

SEPTEMBER						
M	T	W	T	F	S	S
	1	2	3	4	5	6
7	8	9	10	11	12	13
14	15	16	17	18	19	20
21	22	23	24	25	26	27
28	29	30				

OCTOBER						
M	T	W	T	F	S	S
			1	2	3	4
5	6	7	8	9	10	11
12	13	14	15	16	17	18
19	20	21	22	23	24	25
26	27	28	29	30	31	

NOVEMBER						
M	T	W	T	F	S	S
						1
2	3	4	5	6	7	8
9	10	11	12	13	14	15
16	17	18	19	20	21	22
23	24	25	26	27	28	29
30						

DECEMBER						
M	T	W	T	F	S	S
	1	2	3	4	5	6
7	8	9	10	11	12	13
14	15	16	17	18	19	20
21	22	23	24	25	26	27
28	29	30	31			

About the Author

Award-winning astrologer and *Sunday Times* best-selling author Yasmin Boland was born in Germany to English/Irish/Maltese parents and grew up in Hobart, Tasmania. After university, she worked as a journalist, which led her from Tasmania to 'mainland' Australia, and eventually to London, where she worked as a journalist and radio and TV producer.

In the 1990s, learning how to meditate completely changed Yasmin's life and also opened her up to astrology. Her passion for astrology eventually became her profession, and Yasmin is now one of the most widely read astrology writers on the planet. Yasmin loves all astrology but has a special interest in the Moon.

In 2022, Yasmin was voted one of the '100 Most Spiritually Influential Living People.'

Yasmin is the best-selling author of *Moonology™*, *Astrology Made Easy, The Mercury Retrograde Book, Moonology™ Oracle Cards, Moonology™ Manifestation Oracle Cards, Moonology™ Messages Oracle* and the annual *Moonology™ Diary* series.

f **@yasminbolandmoonology**

X **@yasminboland**

@moonologydotcom and **@planetyasminboland**

yasminboland.com and **moonology.com**